CULTURE AND ETHNOLOGY

CULTURE AND ETHNOLOGY

By

ROBERT H. LOWIE, Ph.D.

GYAN

Published by

Gyan Publishing House
5, Ansari Road
Daryaganj, New Delhi-110002
Phone: 011-47034999, 9811692060
E-mail: books@gyanbooks.com

Distribution Network
gyanbooks.com
India, USA, Canada, UK, Australia, France

ISBN : 978-81-212-6478-5 (PB)
First Published, 1917

2nd Impression 2022

Printed at: Gyan Press, Delhi.

CULTURE AND ETHNOLOGY
Author: ROBERT H. LOWIE

CULTURE & ETHNOLOGY

BY

Robert H. Lowie, Ph.D.

1917

CONTENTS

PREFACE

This booklet is an attempt at popularization. The first four chapters are practically identical with as many lectures, delivered in 1917 as the January course offered by the Department of Anthropology of the American Museum of Natural History. The purpose of the January series, which was instituted in 1914 by Dr. P. E. Goddard and the writer, is to acquaint an audience of intelligent laymen with some of the results of modern ethnological work, the emphasis being on principles and problems, rather than on purely descriptive detail. The course, in short, occupies an intermediate position between technical discourses addressed to scientists and the more popular lectures which are designed to furnish mainly entertainment. Each year different topics have been chosen and several members of the staff have cooperated. Owing to the dearth of recent ethnological literature reflecting the position of American field-workers, and at the same time accessible to the interested outsider, I was easily persuaded to issue the 1917 lectures in the present form.

PREFACE

The last chapter may not seem to fit within the scope of this publication. It is obviously more technical than the rest in treatment and may appear to deal with too special a topic. My object, however, was to conclude with a concrete illustration of ethnological method, and I naturally selected a subject to which I had paid considerable attention during the last two years. It is a subject in which Morgan was able to arouse the interest of hundreds of laymen; and I can see no reason why an up-to-date exposition of the problems involved should not be able to hold their attention.

ROBERT H. LOWIE

May, 1917

I. CULTURE AND PSYCHOLOGY[1]

With the beginning of the European war the word 'culture' acquired a sense in popular English usage which had long prevailed in ethnological literature. Culture is, indeed, the sole and exclusive subject-matter of ethnology, as consciousness is the subject-matter of psychology, life of biology, electricity of a branch of physics. Culture shares with these other fundamental concepts the peculiarity that it can be properly understood only by an enlarged familiarity with the facts it summarizes. There is no royal shortcut to a comprehension of culture as a whole by definition any more than to a comprehension of consciousness; but as every analysis and explanation of particular conscious states adds to our knowledge of what consciousness is, so every explanation of particular cultural phenomena adds to our insight into the nature of culture. We must, however, start with some proximate notion of what we are to discuss, and for this purpose Tylor's definition in the opening sentence of his *Primitive Culture* will do as well as any: "Culture . . . is that complex whole which includes knowledge, belief, art, morals, law, custom, and any other capabilities and habits acquired by man as a member of society."

For purely practical reasons, connected with the minute division of labor that has become imperative with modern specialization, ethnology has in practice concerned itself with the cruder cultures of peoples without a knowledge of writing. But this division is an illogical and artificial one. As the biologist can study life as manifested in the human organism as well as in the amoeba, so the ethnologist might examine and describe the usages of modern America as well as those of the Hopi Indians. In these lectures I shall therefore not hesitate to draw upon illustrations from the higher civilizations where these seem most appropriate.

Indeed, it may be best for pedagogical reasons to commence with an enumeration of instances of cultural activity in our own midst. And since there is a persistent tendency to associate with culture the more impressive phenomena of art, science, and technology, it is well to insist at the outset that these loftier phases are by no means necessary to the concept of culture. The fact that your boy plays 'button, button, who has the button?' is just as much an element of our culture as the fact that a room is lighted by electricity. So is the baseball enthusiasm of our grown-up population, so are moving picture shows, *thés dansants*, Thanksgiving Day masquerades, bar-rooms, Ziegfeld Midnight Follies, evening schools, the Hearst papers, woman suffrage clubs, the single-tax movement, Riker drug stores, touring-sedans, and Tammany Hall.

These, then, represent the type of phenomena comprised under the caption of culture. They exist, and science, as a complete view of reality, cannot ignore them. But a question ominous for the worker who derives his bread and butter from ethnological investigation arises. All the phenomena mentioned and the rest of the same order relate to man, and they relate to man not as an animal but as an organism endowed with a higher mentality. Tylor's definition expressly speaks of 'capabilities and habits'. But there *is* a science that deals with capabilities and habits, to wit, psychology. Is it, then, necessary to have a distinct branch of knowledge, or can we not simply merge the cultural phenomena in those of the older science of psychology? It is this question that concerns us here. On the answer must depend our conception of culture and our attitude towards a science purporting to deal with cultural phenomena as something distinct from other data of reality.

In seeking light on this subject we must understand what sort of problems arise from the contemplation of cultural facts and attempt to connect them with the established principles of psychology. A few concrete examples will illustrate the situation.

One of the striking characteristics of our civilization, a trait of our material culture that is nevertheless an invaluable, nay indispensable, means for the propagation of knowledge under modern conditions, is the existence of paper, that is, of a cheap, readily manufactured material for writing and printing. The obvious problem that develops from this fact is, How did we get the art of paper-manufacture? Now we shall search in vain our psychological literature in quest of an explanation. Höffding and James, Wundt and Titchener have no answer to offer. An answer, nevertheless, exists. Europe learnt the art of paper-making from the Arabs, who as early as 795 A.D. had established a paper factory in Bagdad. These in turn got their knowledge from the Chinese, who must be regarded as the originators of the technique. The answer is a perfectly satisfactory one, but it is obviously not couched in psychological terms: its nature is purely *historical*.

Nevertheless, an objection may plausibly be raised here. Though an explanation has certainly been given, it does not account for all aspects of the phenomena we are considering. There *is* a psychological basis for each and every one of the events in our historical series. This series we may subdivide into three stages—the invention by the Chinese, the borrowing of this invention by the Arabs, and its transmission from Arab to European. Now the two last-named processes of transmission may not suggest the necessity of a special explanation at all. One may think that all that was required was for the Europeans to watch the Arabs and for the Arabs to watch the Chinese, and presto! the thing was done. This indeed, seems to be the view of an influential school of modern ethnologists. But the case is far from being so simple. We know of many instances, in the higher no less than in the lower cultures, corresponding to what the biologist calls symbiosis—a condition where distinct communities or countries persist in a division of labor for mutual benefit, each trading some of its intellectual or material products for equivalents secured from the other. In many parts of Africa there are fixed markets in which negroes from fairly remote localities congregate for the barter of wares, which are thus diffused far from their source of origin; but it is the finished products, not the arts, that are diffused. In New Guinea trading-vessels carry such objects as pottery hundreds of miles from the area of manufacture to natives who remain as ignorant of the ceramic technique as before. In northern Arizona the Hopi Indians occupying three eminences not more than eight miles distant from one another have no perfect uniformity of industrial knowledge. Pottery, which flourishes on the eastern Mesa, is wholly unknown as an art, though constantly used in its specimens, by the people of the central Mesa; a certain type of basketry plaque is made only at Oraibi village; another type is manufactured exclusively on the central Mesa. Conditions more ideal *a priori* for a transfer of knowledge than among the practically homogeneous neighboring Hopi groups could not be conceived. Nevertheless, it has not taken place. Cultural diffusion, therefore, cannot be taken for granted. We cannot take one people, place it alongside of another, and effect a cultural osmosis in the same way in which we produce a chemical reaction when two substances are brought together under proper conditions of temperature. We are face to face with a selective, with a *psychological* condition. But when we turn once more to our text-books of psychology, we again find nothing that fits the case. About choice in general we get ample information. But we may rummage all the psychological seminar rooms in the world and yet shall find no reason why the Arabs learned the technique of paper-making from the Chinese instead of ignoring it or only importing Chinese paper.

Nor are we more fortunate when we turn to psychology for an account of how the original Chinese inventor came to conceive his epoch-making idea. This fact, of course, falls under the heading of 'imagination', and about imagination psychologists have much to tell us. But what, after all, does their interpretation amount to? We learn that imagination, as distinguished from the power of abstract thought, is the power of forming new concrete ideas. Since even the concrete individual idea is complex, being a product of association, its elements may be linked differently so as to produce new combinations. "The inventor of a new mechanism," says Höffding, "combines given elements, the laws of whose activity he knows, into a totality and a connection which has no complete parallel in experience." The scientist tries all possible combinations among his elements of experiences, forming a succession of individual ideas, which are rejected until the one appears that adequately represents reality.

We need hardly go farther to realize the impotence of psychological science for illuminating the *psychology* as well as the history of the paper-making art. The formulation of psychological science is admirable, but it is too general. It explains the invention of the steam-engine and the phonograph, the sewing-machine and the harvester no less than the origin of paper-making. We, however, do not want to know merely what ultimate psychological processes the invention of paper-making shares with all other inventions whatsoever, but also the *differential* conditions that produced this one and unique result under the given circumstances. It is as though we asked about a man's character and were told that he was a vertebrate. The type of psychological explanation we want is by no means unknown; however, we shall find its illustrations not in text-books of psychology, but in histories of literature, science, and art. When Taine raises the question how such a bore as Dr. Samuel Johnson could conceivably have attained his position in English literature and answers that it is because of the English predilection for sermons, he is giving the type of solution—whether right or wrong—that we want to secure for our cultural problem; it explains why the average Englishman, as a member of English society, acquires the habit of regarding Johnson in a certain way. When we inquire why Newton closes his treatise on optics with a statement as to the vanity of human things, our curiosity is satisfied when this expression appears as only one instance of the blending of theological and scientific thought current in his day. It is nonsense to say that these explanations are purely historical; they are psychological, for they take fully into account the subjective attitudes involved in the phenomena studied; and it is hopeless to expect this sort of explanation from psychological science, which deals with a quite distinct and far more generalized form of mental activity.

To turn from the technique of paper manufacture to a very different cultural feature in order to test the possibility of merging the observed phenomena in the principles of psychology. In several parts of the globe, and most prominently in parts of South America, the aborigines practise a custom known as the 'couvade', which forces the father of a new-born child to subject himself to a period of inactive confinement and a series of rigorously observed dietary and other regulations. Let us, for the sake of bringing out the point in high relief, ignore all historical considerations and concentrate exclusively on the subjective elements involved. Whence, then, this strange and wholly irrational association of ideas between fatherhood and a group of taboos? Now the subject of the association of ideas occupies hundreds of pages in psychological literature, yet all this, in itself valuable enough, material has no bearing on our problem, because it is again far too general. We do not doubt for a moment that the association we desire to have illuminated is due either to contiguity or to a perceived similarity of ideas, but why have we this particular association instead of the limitless multitude of associations that would be equally intelligible by the same formulae?

Again, many aboriginal tribes of Australia are subdivided into two halves, membership in which is inherited through the father, in some cases, through the mother in others. These moieties are what is technically called 'exogamous', *i.e.*, marriage with a fellow-member is strictly forbidden. The regulation is, indeed, so stringent, the feeling of horror evoked by a transgression so violent, that in former times offenders were promptly put to death. This sentiment is so strong that even when visiting a remote tribe, perhaps a hundred miles away, where there is no possibility of blood-kinship, an Australian will avoid marriage with a member of the moiety bearing the same name as his own. Here, surely, there is matter for psychology. An Australian has a violent emotional reaction akin to our aversion to incest, and may translate his feelings into the most violent action. Or, looking at the matter from another angle, the Australian exercises an admirable self-control, eschewing on principle marital relations with half the women of his community. Yet all that psychologists tell us of the ethical feelings and the will leaves the problem before us wholly untouched. Why this particular curious feeling developed, what place it occupies in mental life, the psychologist fails to explain. We get, again, simply general formulæ about feeling and will that are equally applicable to the case of a man's beating his wife or a boy's resisting the temptations of a lollypop. And this, it must be noted, is dealing with the distinctively psychological aspect of the data. Whether the rule in question originated in a common center and thence spread to other tribes, is also a cultural question of great importance, and this historical phase of the subject psychology is avowedly incompetent to deal with. Psychology, then, fails throughout to supply us with the interpretation we want. It is as impotent to reduce to really interpretative psychological principles the subjective aspect of cultural phenomena as it is to explain the historical sequence of events.

It is not necessary to multiply examples to establish the point. It is clear that cultural phenomena contain elements that cannot be reduced to psychological principles. The reason for the insufficiency is already embodied in Tylor's definition of culture as embracing 'capabilities and habits *acquired* by man as a member of *society*'. The science of psychology, even in its most modern ramifications of abnormal psychology and the study of individual variations, does not grapple with *acquired* mental traits nor with the influence of *society* on individual thought, feeling and will. It deals on principle exclusively with *innate* traits of the *individual*. Now, whether the sharp separation assumed here between the innate and the acquired, between individual activity as determined by uniquely individual potentialities and as determined by social environment, can be made in practice or not, one thing is clear: there *are* phenomena that are acquired and in no sense innate, that are socially and not individually determined. When a Christian reacts in a definite way to the perception of a cross, it is clearly not because of an individual psychic peculiarity, for other Christians react in the same way. On the other hand, we are not dealing with a general human trait since the reactions of a Mohammedan or a Buddhist will be quite different. Innumerable instances of this sort show that individual thought, feeling and volition are co-determined by social influences. In so far forth as the potency of these social factors extends we have culture; in so far forth as knowledge, emotion, and will are neither the result of natural endowment shared with other members of the species nor rest on an individual organic basis, we have a thing *sui generis* that demands for its investigation a distinct science.

Does it follow from the foregoing that there is no possible relation between psychology and culture, that psychological results are a matter of utter indifference to the ethnologist? In their desire to vindicate for their own branch of knowledge a place in the sun, some ethnologists have come very near, if they have not actually reached such a conclusion. To me the case appears in a somewhat different light. Whatever division of labor may be desirable for the economy of scientific work, knowledge as a whole knows nothing of watertight compartments. Further, the nominally distinct sciences are not subordinated to one another, but coexist in a condition of democratic equality and coöperativeness. We cannot reduce cultural to psychological phenomena any more than we can reduce biology to mechanics or chemistry, because in either case the very facts we desire to have explained are ignored in the more generalized formulation. But for specific purposes, the student of culture can call for aid upon each and all of the other branches of learning. It is a very important cultural problem whether the natives of South America knew the bronze technique, *i.e.*, whether they consciously produced the observed alloy of copper and tin. But how can the ethnologist solve this problem? Only by requisitioning the services of the chemist.

Now very few would deny that services of the kind rendered by chemistry can also be rendered to the study of culture by psychology. Indeed, most people would at once admit that the relationship with psychology is *a priori* likely to be far more extensive and thorough-going. A few concrete examples will illustrate how this relationship may be conceived.

Among the quaint conceits with which primitive cultures abound is that of attaching to particular numbers a peculiar character of sanctity. "Everything in the universe," a Crow Indian once told me, "goes by fours." As a matter of fact, most things in Crow religious life are adjusted to this conception. An important ceremonial act is thrice feigned so as to be actually performed at the fourth attempt;

religious processions halt four times; songs are sung in sets of four; in mythic tales it is the fourth trial that carries an heroic feat to a successful issue. Now this cultural fact very largely eludes psychological interpretation. The first thing that strikes us is that this feature is no peculiarity of the Crow, but is rather widely distributed among their immediate neighbors and even remote Indian tribes, though jointly occupying a continuous area. Since outside of this region other numbers figure as mystic, we cannot regard the view of the sacredness of Four as a general trait of human psychology but must assume that the concept was borrowed by most of the tribes now holding it. A wider survey teaches us that corresponding, though not identical, conceptions are very common. *Seven* figures in parts of Asia, *Three* in European folklore, *Five* in Oregon and northern Nevada, *Six* among the Ainu of Yezo, *Nine* among the Yakut, *Ten* among the Pythagorean philosophers of ancient Greece, very much as *Four* does among the Crow. Now the fact that a particular Crow Indian regards Four as a sacred number does not mean that this is an individual peculiarity of his any more than the Christian's reaction to a cross is a proof of some psychological idiosyncrasy. Individually the Crow Indian may be quite indifferent to the number and yet he would view it as sacred because he has been taught so to regard it. This is, of course, the vital difference between ethnology and psychology which has already been emphasized. Nevertheless, the association must at one time have been formed in an individual mind, whether among the Crow or elsewhere, and the question arises as to what such an association means. Francis Galton showed some time ago that such associations of definite personal characteristics with numbers occur by no means infrequently among Europeans. The phenomenon we are dealing with is thus linked with a group of related phenomena and in so far forth is explained.

There are ethnologists who would not admit that such an explanation has anything to do with ethnology. They would contend that as soon as we cease to investigate the group as such we are passing from ethnology, the science of culture, to psychology, the science of individual minds. This seems an unnecessarily narrow doctrinaire view. Knowledge, as stated above, is not subdivided by hard-and-fast partitions. Interest certainly does not stop at an arbitrary point in the investigation but is centered on a comprehension of the *whole* phenomenon. Where that phenomenon is an alloy of tin and copper, a decision as to its nature is naturally left to chemistry; it seems not unreasonable that where it is a type of association we should turn for enlightenment to psychology.

Another field supplies an additional illustration. One of the important subjects for ethnographic study is artistic form. The ethnologist notes in a purely descriptive way the decorative patterns employed by various tribes, the fact that curvilinear motives are prominent among the Maori of New Zealand while the rawhide bags of Plains Indians are covered with angular paintings. Here, once more, it is clear that many of the problems that arise are purely cultural. There are, nevertheless, psychological elements involved that may be misunderstood without psychological knowledge. Let us assume, *e. g.*, that a certain tribe is artistically characterized by a fondness for squares. What does this predilection signify? It is a psychological commonplace that through an optical illusion we exaggerate the height as compared with the width of a rectangle; accordingly, the geometrical square does not coincide with the psychological square. This simple piece of information enables us to understand *what* we are actually dealing with in the case of a square pattern. At the same time it sharpens our observation regarding such patterns. It is quite conceivable that in one place tribal taste should prefer the actual square while elsewhere the psychological square occupies the seat of honor. This would be a purely ethnographic fact, yet its discovery might be considerably expedited by some knowledge of experimental aesthetics.

Let us turn from mystic numbers and decorative designs to another aspect of primitive life. The Turkish tribes of western Siberia have a form of religion based on the belief that certain individuals enjoy the hereditary privilege of acting as intermediaries between their ancestral spirits and the people at large. With the aid of his sacred drum the shaman, as such an intermediary is technically called, is able to summon the supernatural beings, cure the sick, foretell the future, separate his own soul from his body and send it to the upper realms of light or the nether regions of darkness. Now, although a particular individual inherits the shaman's office from his father, he receives no formal instruction nor does he make any active preparation for his mission. His call comes in the form of a sudden paroxysm. He is seized with a feeling of languor and a fit of violent convulsions, with abnormal yawning, and a powerful pressure on the chest, which causes him to utter inarticulate screams. He begins to shiver with cold, rolls his eyes, suddenly leaps up and madly circles about until he falls down covered with perspiration and writhing in epileptic spasms on the ground. His members are devoid of sensation, his hands grasp without discrimination red-hot iron, knives, pins; he swallows such objects without suffering the slightest injury, and again ejects them from his mouth. Finally, the prospective seer seizes a shaman's drum and assumes the shaman's office. Disobedience to the spirit's call would spell disaster, madness and death amidst the most horrible tortures.[2]

The naïve reaction to this narrative on the part of common sense in the familiar form of common ignorance will probably be that the European traveler who is our authority is a very gullible individual if he believed his native informant's statements. How can an individual be seized with such a spasm as that described? How is it possible for him to become devoid of sensation? Nevertheless, nothing is more certain than that the account given is substantially correct. It is simply a particular form of nervous affliction very common throughout Siberia and attested by dozens of trustworthy eyewitnesses.[3] This Arctic hysteria, as it has been misnamed (for there is nothing distinctively Arctic about it), manifests itself principally in two ways. Either the individual falls victim to an indiscriminate mania for mimicking the acts of others; or he is seized with the sort of paroxysm described for the Turkish shaman. Nothing is clearer than that in neither case is there usually conscious deception. Sometimes the imitation mania subjects the sufferer to ridicule and pain, as when an old woman in imitation of a Cossack, seized a salmon with her teeth, ran up a hill and down again, unable to prevent herself from plunging into the water, though normally she was barely able to walk. Similarly, the numerous hysterical individuals of the other type who do not become inspired shamans cannot possibly derive any benefit from their fits.

Abnormal psychology here steps in and teaches us that such trances are involuntary and not the result of fraud, that they occur in our own civilization and are accompanied with extraordinary lack of sensibility to pain, in short, psychiatry classifies the observed phenomena and tells us what we are really dealing with. It prevents a misconception alike of the shaman's activities and of the attitude of his people towards him.

When, however, abnormal psychology has so far enlightened us, it has by no means exhausted even the purely subjective aspect of the case. How does the prospective shaman seized with his fit know about the shamanistic drum that forms a necessary accessory of his office? How does he know what mode of activity is expected from him? These are *not* things which he can get directly from his trance for we shall hardly accept the aboriginal theory that he is inspired by the ancestral spirits. He can derive his knowledge, however informally, only as the member of a group holding certain definite views as to the shamanistic office. The cultural phenomenon, then, even on its psychological side, comprises a very appreciable *plus* over and above the facts that psychology can explain, and these additional data accordingly require treatment by another science.

My conclusions as to the relation of psychology to culture are, accordingly, the following: The cultural facts, even in their subjective aspect, are not merged in psychological facts. They must not, indeed, contravene psychological principles, but the same applies to all other principles of the universe; culture cannot construct houses contrary to the laws of gravitation nor produce bread out of stones. But the principles of psychology are as incapable of accounting for the phenomena of culture as is gravitation to account for architectural styles. Over and above the interpretations given by psychology, there is an irreducible residuum of huge magnitude that calls for special treatment and by its very existence vindicates the *raison d'être* of ethnology. We need not eschew any help given by scientific psychology for the comprehension of specifically psychological components of cultural phenomena; but as no one dreams of saying that these phenomena are reduced to chemical principles when chemistry furnishes us with an analysis of Peruvian bronze implements, so no one can dare assert that they are reduced to psychological principles when we call upon psychology to elucidate specific features of cultural complexes. The 'capabilities and habits acquired by man as a member of society' constitute a distinct aspect of reality that must be the field of a distinct science autonomous with reference to psychology.

II. CULTURE AND RACE

If culture is a complex of socially acquired traits, it might appear that race could not possibly have any influence on culture, since by racial characteristics we understand those which are innate by virtue of ancestry. This, however, by no means follows. In order that certain traits be acquired, a certain type of organic basis is an absolute prerequisite; a chimpanzee or a bat is not able to acquire human culture through social environment. From an evolutionary point of view it appears, therefore, very plausible at first blush that within the human species, likewise, differences in organization should be correlated with the observed cultural manifestations of varying degree and complexity. There was, undoubtedly, some stage in human evolution where the organic basis for culture had not yet been acquired. Can the several races be regarded as transitional forms, each possessed of certain capabilities determining and limiting its cultural achievement? This question can be viewed in two ways. Comparative psychology may give us direct information as to qualitative and quantitative racial differences that would affect cultural activity. Or, we may infer such differences as the only possible causes for the observed cultural differences. Both modes of approach are helpful for a comprehension of the problem.

Until recent years the psychological evaluation of primitive tribes rested largely on the offhand judgments of travelers and missionaries. With the advent of more exact psychological laboratory methods, these have been, in some measure, applied by competent investigators to aboriginal populations. Unfortunately, the results hitherto secured are somewhat meager. There are technical difficulties, among them the necessity of examining fairly large numbers of individuals in order to get a good sample of the population. Worse still, laboratory methods are most effective in regard to what may be called the lower mental operations, which partake almost more of a physiological than of a strictly psychological character. Clearly enough, what we should be most desirous of knowing is how primitive compares with civilized man in logical thought and imagination. But these are precisely the things not readily tested, and here the additional technical difficulty comes in that they can hardly be examined at all without a far more intimate knowledge of the native languages than the investigator is likely to command. Nevertheless, something has been done and I will attempt to present as briefly as possible the essential results, following Thorndike's convenient summary.[1]

Although some observers have attributed unusual acuity of sense perception to the more primitive peoples of the globe, the investigations of Rivers, Woodworth, and others in the main establish the psychic unity of mankind in this regard. For example, though the Kalmuk are renowned for their vision, only one or two of the individuals tested exceeded the European record, and while Bruner found Indians and Filipino inferior in hearing a watch tick or a click transmitted by telephone, the fairness of these tests for natives unused to such stimuli has been reasonably challenged. In their reaction-time tests, widely different groups were very similar. In the tapping test, measuring the rate at which the brain can at will discharge a series of impulses to the same muscle, marked differences were also lacking; but when accuracy as well as rapidity were examined, the Filipino seemed decidedly superior to the whites. Optical illusions were shared by all races tested, which indicates, as Woodworth points out, that simple sorts of judgments as well as sensory processes are common to the generality of mankind. Woodworth subjected his subjects to an intelligence test, demanding that blocks of different shapes be fitted into a board with holes to match the blocks. In speed the average differences between whites, Indians, Eskimo, Ainu, Filipino, and Singhalese are small and there is considerable overlapping. On the other hand, the Igorrote and Philippine Negrito, as well as a group of supposed Pygmies from the Congo, proved remarkably deficient. "This crumb," concludes our investigator, "is about all the testing psychologist has yet to offer on the question of racial differences in intelligence."

It may well be, as Thorndike suggests, that if higher functions were studied, more striking differences would be revealed. But up to date we can simply say that experimental psychological methods have revealed no far-reaching differences in the mental processes of the several races. Even the Igorrote and Negrito deficiency may be due, Woodworth suggests, to their habits of life rather than to their native endowment.

Since exact methods tell us nothing of those higher operations we are most eager to know about, it might be deemed advisable to fall back on general estimates by the most competent observers. Unfortunately, the personal equation enters here to an extent that completely nullifies the value of individual judgments. Travelers in foreign lands are likely to make quite unusual demands on the capacities of the natives with whose aid they are working, and in this way too frequently arrive at an unfair conclusion as to their mental characteristics. In a corresponding test Europeans might do little better. It is, at all events, remarkable that unbiased observers who are fairly sympathetic and remain in long contact with a primitive people usually entertain a rather favorable opinion of their powers. Thus, Prince Maximilian of Wied-Neuwied, expresses the view that, whether other varieties of mankind differ or not, the American aborigines are not inferior to the whites,[2] and corresponding estimates have been made of other races. Still, these are merely personal opinions and we must turn to our second method for possibly more objective, if indirect, evidence on the subject. Are, then, cultural differences necessarily the result of racial differences?

In thus investigating the relations between race and civilization we may fruitfully employ the method of variation. Making the racial factor a constant, we may inquire whether culture, too, is thereby made a constant, and whether a change in racial propinquity is correlated with a proportionate change of culture. On the other hand, we may start with culture as a constant and inquire whether each form or grade of culture is the concomitant of definite racial characteristics and whether a change in culture is accompanied by a corresponding change of race.

To begin with the latter method, which may be briefly disposed of: Taking our own type of culture, as represented in western Europe and North America, we find that it is shared by at least one people of quite distinct stock, the Japanese, who have already made important contributions to the general civilization of the world in such lines as biology and scientific medicine. An obvious objection is that the Japanese are not the originators of our cultural foundation but have borrowed it ready-made (as they once borrowed that of China), and merely added a few additional stones to the superstructure. This fact cannot, of course, be questioned, but as soon as we investigate historically the origin of our own modern civilization we find that it, too, is largely the product of numerous cultural streams, some of which may be definitely traced to distinct races or sub-races. Our immediate indebtedness to Rome and Greece has been drilled into us with such fulsomely exaggerated emphasis in our schooldays that the less said about it the better for a fair estimate of general culture history. That the Greeks were merely the continuators and inheritors of an earlier Oriental culture, must be considered an established fact. Our economic life, based as it is on the agricultural employment of certain cereals with the aid of certain domesticated animals, is derived from Asia; so is the technologically invaluable wheel.[3] The domestication of the horse certainly originated in inner Asia; modern astronomy rests on that of the Babylonians, Hindu, and Egyptians; the invention of glass is an Egyptian contribution; spectacles come from India;[4] paper, to mention only one other significant element of our civilization, was borrowed from China. What is right for the goose, is right for the gander; and if the Japanese deserve no credit for having appropriated our culture, we must also carefully eliminate from that culture all elements not demonstrably due to the creative genius of our race before laying claim to the residue as our distinctive product. As Thorndike, among others, has pointed out,[5] the races have not remained in splendid isolation, but any particular one has obtained most of its civilization from without, and "of ten equally gifted races in perfect intercourse each will originate only one-tenth of what it gets." This, to be sure, represents an ideal condition, and we have no right to assume gratuitously that the peoples in contact are all equally gifted; but it is worth noting that momentous ideas may be conceived by what we are used to regard as inferior races. Thus, the Maya of Central America conceived the notion of the zero figure, which remained unknown to Europeans until they borrowed it from India; and eminent ethnologists suggest that the discovery of the iron technique is due to the Negroes.

In short, the possessors of a culture are not necessarily its originators; often they are demonstrably borrowers of specific elements of the greatest significance. The same culture may thus become the property of distinct races, as is rapidly becoming the case in modern times. Owing to the very extensive occurrence of diffusion the question what a particular people or race has originated becomes extremely complicated; while it is an established fact that important additions to human civilization have been made by diverse stocks.

It may not be out of place to point out that not only the more tangible elements of culture, but very much subtler ingredients than those hitherto mentioned are shared by distinct groups of mankind. Thus, common to ourselves and the

Chinese, though strikingly lacking among the Hindu, who, nevertheless, are racially nearer to us, is a marked sense for historical perspective. Common to the ancient Romans, the modern Germans, and the modern Japanese, is the talent for rationalistic organization of administrative affairs. We cannot assume under the circumstances that the Japanese are organically nearer to the Germans than to other Asiatics. These instances seem the more valuable because here borrowing is excluded. The racial factor may in some way be involved; it is conceivable that only with a certain minimum of organic equipment could a particular cultural trait be developed or even assimilated. But obviously the same cultural traits may be coupled with different racial characteristics.

But what results from making race a constant? That no essential organic change has taken place in the human race during the historic period is universally admitted without question by biologists, physical anthropologists, and brain specialists. Accordingly, when we concentrate our attention on a definite people and follow their fortunes during historic times, we are dealing with a genuine constant from the racial point of view. It requires no very great acquaintance with history to note startling cultural diversity correlated with this stability of organic endowment.

The culture of the Mongol proper about the beginning of the thirteenth century was that of an essentially primitive people, sharing the shamanistic beliefs of their general habitat and ignorant of writing. Suddenly we find them attaining an extraordinary political importance, dominating Asia and menacing Europe, conversant successively with several forms of script, practising the art of printing, and becoming ardent exponents of Buddhism. Today they appear fallen from their high estate, devoid of political power, and with their semi-sedentary nomad life again give the impression of primitiveness, though tempered with evidences of a higher civilization.[6] These changes are not only manifestly independent of the racial factor, but can in part be directly traced to other causes. Buddhism, of course, was derived ultimately from India. Under Jenghis Khan both Chinese characters and an alphabet derived from the Syrian, which had been spread through central Asia by Nestorian missionaries, came into use; while another system of writing was based on that of Tibet, and the art of printing was learned from the Chinese.[7] The political predominance of the Mongols was due to a few powerful personalities;

and economic factors seem to have been at least potent agents in the degenerative process of Mongol civilization. In short, we have a group of determinants that are not even remotely connected with hereditary racial traits.

Somewhat similar results appear from a consideration of Manchu history. The Manchu were originally an insignificant and rude tribe of the Tungusic family in eastern Siberia. Through contact with the Mongols they became a literary people. They subjected China in 1644, and adopted the Chinese speech and mode of thinking to such an extent that their language is no longer spoken and almost every vestige of their former lore is irretrievably lost.[8]

An equally striking illustration is furnished by the Arabs. Here, too, we have a people of crude civilization suddenly emerging from an unimportant position in the world's affairs to blossom forth not only as a military and political, but a cultural power as well, deriving from Persia and Babylonia the impulse to philological and historical studies, from Byzantium the technique of naval warfare, the art of paper-manufacture from the Chinese, Euclid from the Syrian outposts of Greek culture, and from India the decimal notation.[9] We find further that they were not passive assimilators, but original elaborators and active transmitters of the received elements, to whom European science is under a lasting debt of gratitude and whose art constitutes at least a highly creditable and individual achievement.

The conclusion suggested by these examples is very strongly corroborated by an examination of our own race. We need not enter into the subtleties of sub-racial classifications for the present purpose, but will simply regard the European race in relation to European culture generally. It is clear that all those startling technological advantages that most sharply divide us from other peoples are a mushroom growth little over a century old. In the first half of the nineteenth century matches were unknown and the processes of fire-making were not superior to those of many primitive tribes. The steam-engine and the industrial revolution are of very little greater antiquity, not to speak of electrical contrivances and applied chemistry. The difference between ourselves and our forefathers is at first blush so tremendous that *a priori* it would seem to be explainable only by very great mental differences, yet nothing is more certain than that their innate mentality was exactly the same. The cultural difference becomes more and more glaring as we proceed backwards, say, to the period antedating the art of printing. A portion of our

Middle Ages compares rather unfavorably with contemporaneous Arabian or Chinese civilization. "If we go back to the fifteenth century," says Professor Giles, "we shall find that the standard of civilization, as the term is usually understood, was still much higher in China than in Europe; while Marco Polo, the famous Venetian traveler of the thirteenth century, who actually lived twenty-four years in China, and served as an official under Kublai Khan, has left it on record that the magnificence of Chinese cities, and the splendor of the Chinese court, outrivaled anything he had ever seen or heard of."[10]

Certainly the racial factor, which is a constant, cannot account for the amazing changes in culture which we encounter in passing from one period of our era to another. If we are interested in explaining these cultural phenomena, we must cast about for some other determinants.

In a subject that is constantly confused by partisanship it is important to make no greater claims for an argument than the facts absolutely warrant. Accordingly, I hasten to explain what has really been shown and what I have failed to show hitherto. It is, I think, fair to say that culture cannot be adequately explained by race, and that the same race varies extraordinarily in culture even within a very narrow space of time. But we have not furnished proof that, say, the Central African Pygmies, the Tasmanians, or the aborigines of Australia would have been capable of attaining unaided to the level of our civilization. What we can say, however, is this: The Chinese and some of our American Indians, such as the ancient Central Americans and Peruvians, did attain a very high level, which may be equated with that of Europe at a relatively recent period. The difference between European culture then and now cannot be due to hereditary causes, and it would, therefore, be unjustifiable to allege that such causes account for the difference between Europe of today and China or ancient Central America. Quite generally it is true that the so-called primitive tribes are anything but primitive in the strict sense of the term. Ingenious contrivances, such as the boomerang, occur among the Australians, usually regarded as one of the lowliest of races, and here we also find a remarkable complexity of social organization. The Negroes of Africa are not only conversant with the art of metallurgy, which is possibly their own invention, but are conspicuous for their ability to form large and powerful political states and have shown at least the ability of assimilating the culture of Islam.

If we contrast Negro culture on the average not with the highest products of Dutch, Danish, or Swiss culture, but with the status of the illiterate peasant communities in not a few regions of Europe, the difference will hardly be so great as to suggest any far-reaching hereditary causes. As the highly civilized Manchu of today have for their next racial kin very crude Siberian populations, so the white race, even today, embraces very primitive as well as highly advanced constituent groups. We cannot wholly isolate the racial factor from others, and we cannot give an ocular demonstration of what the several inferior races, so-called, are capable of achieving under the most favorable conditions. But with great confidence we can say that since the same race at different times or in different subdivisions at the same time represents vastly different cultural stages, there is obviously no direct *proportional* relation between culture and race. And if great changes of culture can occur without any change of race whatsoever, we are justified in considering it probable that a relatively minute change of hereditary ability might produce enormous differences. An analogy may render the matter clearer. Suppose that it is of vital importance to lift a heavy weight, say 400 pounds, to which only a single individual has access at the same time. Then a very slight difference in muscular power will either accomplish or fail in producing the desired effect, and the ultimate effect (say in repelling an attack on a fortress under relatively primitive conditions) will be entirely incommensurate with the additional strength required to produce it. So we may readily understand how a slightly greater mechanical aptitude might render one race able to launch a remarkable series of inventions for which another, by barely missing the required degree of development, would be forever debarred. This is only a special form of the Darwinian doctrine of the survival value of small variations, applied not to the question of the struggle for existence (with which, nevertheless, it may be most intimately related), but to the creation of new cultural values.

This aspect of the subject naturally leads to another that is closely connected with it and is essential to an understanding of the entire question. Mental endowment is a variable phenomenon within any particular people or tribe. However democratic may be our ideals, the doctrine that all individuals are born equal in point of ability can no longer be seriously maintained. Every race must, therefore, be regarded not as representing a single point of mental development, but as a continuum of mental values with a certain range of variation. In comparing the different races we must, accordingly, apply the canons used by statisticians in comparing series of variable measurements. Here a matter of vital importance challenges our attention. Two series may have the same average value and yet differ considerably in range. Now it is obvious that, where the number of individuals considered is small, excessive values are less likely to occur than in a larger series. In a gathering of a hundred men, we are not likely to find a man above 6 feet 6 inches in height; the average stature of all New Yorkers will probably not be any greater than that of one hundred men selected at random, yet in the entire city we shall find a number of individuals of gigantic stature. When we apply this fact to our special problem we see at once that extraordinary deviations from the norm cannot be expected to occur in a tribe of 500 or even 5,000, while among the vast populations of India, China or the Caucasian countries of America and Europe such favorable variants are likely to occur with considerable absolute frequency. These variations, as has already been suggested, need not even be excessive to produce significant cultural results. Again, we may urge the principle of minimal variations.

A *little* greater energy or administrative talent may be just sufficient to found a powerful state; a *slightly* greater amount of logical consistency may lead to the foundation of geometrical reasoning or of a philosophical system; a *somewhat* keener interest, above the purely utilitarian one, in surrounding nature may give a remarkable impetus to the development of science.

Now this puts an entirely different construction on the facts. Assume that racial differences *are* at the bottom of some of the observed cultural differences. This fact would not necessarily mean, then, that the *average* ability of the inferior races is less, but only that extreme variations of an advantageous character occur less frequently among them. This, for example, is the view taken by Professor Eugen Fischer, the physical anthropologist, a very firm believer in racial differences, but as regards variability rather than in point of average intellectual equipment. It is also essentially, if I understand him, the point made by Professor Thorndike. But precisely because the population of the several races differs so enormously, we are for many of them without a fair standard of comparison. Statistically, any actual number of measurements is only a small sample of an infinite series; but we have no means of ascertaining empirically what the extreme variations of which Veddas or Australians are organically capable, would be like. This, necessarily, leaves the ultimate problem of racial differences unsolved. Nevertheless, our considerations have not been in vain. They show, for one thing, how many factors have to be weighed in arriving at a fair estimate of racial capabilities, factors which are naïvely ignored in most popular discussions of the subject. We can, farther, say positively that whatever differences may exist have been grossly exaggerated. In the simpler mental operations, comparative psychological studies indicate a specific unity of mankind. Differences in culture are certainly not proportionate to mental differences, *i.e.*, relatively slight differences in native ability may well have produced tremendous cultural effects. Since, finally, cultural differences of enormous range occur within the same race, and even within very much smaller subdivisions, the ethnologist cannot solve his cultural problems by means of the race factor. Even if an ultimate investigation should definitely fix the cultural limits to which a given race is hereditarily subject, such information could not solve the far more specific problem why the same people a few hundred years earlier were a horde of barbarians and a few hundred years later formed a highly civilized community.

The supposed explanation by racial potentialities would be far too general to interpret the actual happenings. Racial psychology, no less than general psychology, thus fails to solve the problems of culture.

III. CULTURE AND ENVIRONMENT[1]

The influence of geographical environment on culture seems a matter not so much of logical inference as of direct observation. Taking our own continent, we know that cotton is raised in the South, that our wheat belt lies in Minnesota and the adjoining states and Canadian provinces, that the Rocky Mountain and some of the Plateau states are the seat of the mining industry while Florida and California form our tropical fruit orchards. With these obvious facts are combined correlations not so clear, perhaps, yet very convincing to the mind as yet undebauched by ethnological learning. What seems more natural than that culture in its highest forms should develop only in temperate regions, that the gloomy forests of the North be reflected in a mythology of ogres and trolls, that liberty should flourish amidst snowy mountain tops and languish in the tepid plain, or that islanders should be expert mariners?

This geographical theory of culture bears a certain resemblance to the classical associationist theory in psychology. According to that doctrine, the mind is something in the nature of a wax tablet on which the outer world produces impressions and all the higher mental activities are, in the last instance, reducible to combinations of the represented impressions or 'ideas'. Modern psychology, however, regards this system, fascinating as it appears at a first glance, as little better than an historical curiosity. The association of ideas itself is now conceived merely as a special manifestation of the synthetic nature of consciousness. In short, the tables are completely turned, and association, instead of explaining consciousness, is interpreted in terms of consciousness. The analogy with the geographical view of culture will become apparent in the course of our discussion.

To begin with the culture of our own country: The environmental features of southern California, of Nevada, and the South have not changed during the last few centuries. Yet, what do we find on considering the aboriginal cultures of these regions? Southern California and Nevada were unreclaimed desert wastes inhabited by a roving, non-agricultural population, the natural mining resources of the latter state remained untouched, no attempt was made to grow cotton in the Southern cotton area. How can such facts be interpreted on a geographical basis? Quite obviously, the reverse holds. The utilization of part of the environment, instead of being an automatic response, has for an indispensable prerequisite a certain type of culture. Granted the existence of an agricultural technique, attempts may be made to apply it even in a forbidding arid climate, where a more primitive culture would not be able to develop it. The unfavorable environment may have checked such development, and in so far forth exerted cultural influence at one stage, but it is unable to check it at another stage, where the preëxisting culture, instead of 'remaining put', molds the environment to its own purposes.

The case I have chosen is an extreme one because I have correlated environment with extremes of culture—one of the lowest forms of aboriginal North American culture and our modern advanced scientific methods of subduing nature to our will. But if we consider only the cruder forms of civilization the same point appears with equal clearness.

Professor Kirchhoff, by no means an extreme adherent of the geographical school since he does not reduce man to a mere automaton in the face of his surroundings, nevertheless believes in a far-reaching influence of the environment and cites in particular the resemblances between inhabitants of arid territories. Unfortunately for his argument we have glaring instances in which desert-like conditions coexist with disparate modes of culture not only in similar but in identical regions of the globe.

Thus, the Hopi and Navajo Indians have both occupied for a long period the same part of northeastern Arizona and on the environmental theory we should therefore expect among them the same mode of life. In this, however, we are thoroughly disappointed. The Hopi are intensive farmers who succeed in raising crops where white agriculturists fail; the Navajo also plant corn but to a distinctly lesser extent and under Spanish influence have readily developed into a pastoral people, raising sheep for food and wool. Though the same building material is available, the Hopi construct the well-known terraced sandstone houses with a rectangular cell as the architectural unit, while the Navajo dwell in conical earth-covered huts. North American ceramic art attains one of its highwater marks among the Hopi, while the pottery of the Navajo is hopelessly crude in comparison. Cotton was raised by the Hopi, but there is no trace of its use by the neighboring people. What is true of the material aspect of native life applies equally to its less tangible elements. There is at least one marked difference in the sexual division of labor: with the Hopi it is the man's business to spin and weave while this work falls to woman's share among the Navajo. The Hopi were always strict monogamists, while among the Navajo polygamy was permissible. In conjunction with their agricultural pursuits Hopi ceremonialism centered in the magico-religious production of rain; the Navajo applied often the identical ritualistic stock-in-trade to the cure of sickness. A stringent regulation of the Navajo social code forbids all conversation between son-in-law and mother-in-law; but the Hopi merely view the taboo as a Navajo idiosyncrasy. The general cast of Hopi psychology, as fashioned by Hopi society, is that of an eminently peaceable population; the Navajo rather recall in their bearing the warlike and aggressive tribes of the Plains. Where resemblances occur, as *e. g.*, in the objective phase of the native cults, we are able to prove that the parallelism is due not to an independent response to environmental stimuli, but to contact and borrowing. But quite apart from such cases, the basic differences in Hopi and Navajo civilization show that the environment alone cannot account for cultural phenomena.

If we pass from the southwestern United States to South Africa, a corresponding situation confronts us. The same area at one time formed the habitat of the Bushmen and the Hottentots; yet, their mode of life varies fundamentally. The Bushmen are essentially hunters and seed-collectors, while the Hottentots are an eminently pastoral people. Caves and crude windbreaks form the Bushman's original dwellings, while the Hottentots have mat-covered portable bee-hive-shaped huts. The Bushman's principal weapons are bow and arrow, with the Hottentot these implements are of secondary importance as compared with the spear. It is true that not only material objects but even myths and folk-tales are shared by both tribes, but in many instances of this sort we have clearly a case not of independent response to the same external conditions but rather the result of borrowing. Thus, some of the traits common to Hottentot and Bushman, for example, a fair number of mythic episodes, occur likewise among the Bantu Negroes inhabiting contiguous but geographically different territory. One of the most interesting traits of ancient Bushman culture is the life-like representation of animals on rocks and the walls of caves. Oddly enough, these engravings and mural paintings, which distinguish the Bushmen from their South African neighbors, have their nearest parallels in the Spanish cave-paintings of Palæolithic Europe.

The picturing of the mammoth and reindeer by these old South European artists clearly proves that they belonged to a glacial epoch, during which geographical conditions could hardly have resembled those of the Kalahari desert.[2]

One other illustration from the same general region of the Dark Continent is suggestive. The Ovambo and Herero, neighbors though they are, differ in the essential features of their economic life. While the Ovambo depend only to a very limited extent on their herds, deriving their sustenance mainly from the cultivation of millet and other plants, the Herero are the only non-agricultural Bantu people, being predominantly pastoral.

Instead of comparing the effect of environment as a whole on different peoples, we can also isolate its single factors, such as the presence of particular species of plants or animals. One of the strongest cases against the creative influence of environment on culture lies in the phenomena relating to the domestication of animals in the Old and the New World. The one animal domesticated in both hemispheres is the dog, which occurs in Neolithic Europe and is also found with archæological remains in America. But while in the Old World there is in addition an imposing series of species subjected to man for definite economic utilization, it is only in Peru that the American natives entered into a symbiotic arrangement with other animals, *viz.*, the llama and the alpaca. Why was not the bison of the great Plains tamed like the buffalo of southern Asia or the various races of cattle in the Eastern Hemisphere? No valid reason can be advanced on geographical grounds. More striking still in this regard is the difference between the hyperborean populations of Asia and North America. The Chukchee of northeasternmost Siberia and the Eskimo share the same climatic conditions and their territories are both inhabited by the reindeer (caribou). Yet the Chukchee breed half-tamed reindeer on a large scale, using the animals for food and draught with sledges, while no attempt in this direction was made by the Eskimo or any of their Indian neighbors. The same external condition fails to produce the same cultural result. But even among the Chukchee there is evidence that the use of reindeer did not take place in response to an environmental stimulus. It appears that the extraordinary development of reindeer breeding is a relatively new thing with the Chukchee, who were formerly hunters of sea-mammals like the Eskimo. Before the recent efflorescence of their reindeer culture, the

Chukchee waged war on their southern neighbors, the Koryak, for the purpose of carrying off their herds; and altogether it seems that both Chukchee and Koryak adopted the idea of taming the reindeer from tribes of the Tungus stock living to the west and south.[3] We are, then, dealing with another instance of acculturation due to contact.

The facts of domestication are unusually suggestive as regards our general problem for they show in an absolutely convincing manner that even where the same animals have been domesticated by different peoples the use to which they are put may differ widely and give a distinct aspect to this phase of culture. Thus, we find that of Siberian reindeer-breeders the Tungus and Lamut use their animals only for transportation, not for slaughter, and that many bands, unlike other Arctic populations, ride on their reindeer instead of harnessing them to sledges. It is true that a rationalistic motive can be given for the fact that the Chukchee do not ride reindeer-back since their variety seems physically unfit for the saddle. That, however, is not the essential point. We should like to know how the Tungus came to use the saddle with their animals while other tribes with the same variety did not do so, and for this *positive* reaction to their faunal environment geography furnishes no clue. A similar group of questions arises in connection with the horse. Wild horses were game animals in Solutrean times in Europe, their flesh forming in fact the staple diet. Domestication certainly set in at a very much later period and its economic consequences vary appreciably with different peoples and in different times. The Kirgis, for example, milk their mares, thus obtaining the famous kumyss, though the operation is difficult and even dangerous.[4] The ancient Babylonians, Chinese, and East Indians used the horse as a draught-animal harnessed to war-chariots. Its use for riding was an invention of Central Asiatic nomads. In the most recent period the consumption of horse flesh is a matter of course among the poorer classes of continental Europe, revolting as the idea is not only to the white American but to some of the Plains Indians as well, according to the testimony of some of my informants. There is thus no such thing as the presence of the horse determining its cultural use in a definite sense.

Again, the ancient Chinese kept both sheep and goats, but the idea of utilizing wool for clothing was foreign to them. We have historical evidence for the fact that the use of wool for felt and rugs was taught to the Chinese in more recent times by the nomadic populations of central Asia. Most startling of all perhaps is the different attitude assumed in different countries towards cattle. To us nothing seems more obvious than that cattle should be kept both for meat and dairy products. This, however, is by no means a universal practice. The Zulu and other Bantu tribes of South Africa use milk extensively but hardly ever slaughter their animals except on festive occasions. On the other hand, we have the even more astonishing fact that Eastern Asiatics, such as the Chinese, Japanese, Koreans and Indo-Chinese, have an inveterate aversion to the use of milk. Though the Chinese, as Dr. Laufer points out, have raised a variety of animals from which milk could be derived and have been in constant contact with Turkish and Mongol nations whose staple food consists in dairy products, they have never acquired what seems so obvious and useful an economic practice. Accordingly, Dr. Laufer justifiably concludes that "our consumption of animal milk cannot be looked upon as a self-evident and spontaneous phenomenon, for which it has long been taken, but that it is a mere matter of educated force of habit."[5] In other words, the use of environmental factors is not an automatic and necessary response to them but varies with the culture of the peoples concerned.

The creative impotence of environment and more particularly the subordinate part it plays as compared with purely cultural determinants of culture, such as the influence of a certain trait in a neighboring tribe or the preëxistence of indigenous cultural features, may be instructively illustrated by several other instances.

Thus, we find that of the Northern Athabaskans of western Canada, the southern Carrier and the Chilcotin Indians share with the Shuswap Indians of Salish stock the use of semi-subterranean huts which even in winter seem like ovens. Are we to recognize in this an adaptation to the inclemencies of the climate? Hardly, when we find that this type of dwelling is used precisely by those Athabaskans living farthest south, where of course the climate is much milder, while the more northern tribes of the family get along with crude double shelters about a central fireplace. The use of the semi-subterranean lodge by the Carrier and Chilcotin is perfectly explained as a contact phenomenon. They have simply adopted the idea from their Salish neighbors: the cultural environment has proved more effective than the physical environment in determining a cultural trait. Other members of the same family furnish corresponding instances. Though many of the Northern Athabaskans have long, snowy winters, only the Loucheux, who are in contact with the Eskimo, have adopted the wooden goggles of the Eskimo, which serve as a protection against snow-blindness. Similarly, they are the only members of the stock to substitute for the widespread Canadian toboggan the Eskimo sledge with runners.[6]

As the physical environment is overshadowed in cultural significance by a neighboring culture, so it may vanish into nothingness in the face of what we may call cultural inertia—the tendency of a preëxisting cultural trait of indigenous growth to assert itself. A familiar example of this tendency is the exact imitation of forms of implements in quite different and often refractory material. Thus, the Central Eskimo generally make lamps and pots out of soapstone. In Southampton Island, where this material is lacking, they have not devised a new form but have at the expenditure of much ingenuity and labor cemented together slabs of limestone so as to produce the traditional shape.[7] The same phenomenon appears in other fields. Grooved copper axes have been found in parts of the

United States; their shape is patterned exactly on the stone axes characteristic of the same localities. The beginnings of the copper and bronze ages in Europe are equally suggestive in this regard. The incipient metallurgist does not automatically make the most of his material but slavishly follows his stone or bone models. His copper ornaments imitate bear's teeth or bone beads, his implements resemble the stone celts and hammers of an earlier era.[8] As Professor Boas points out on the basis of Bogoras' descriptions, an equivalent development may be traced in the history of the Chukchee tent. This type of habitation is extremely clumsy and not at all well adapted to the roving life of the Reindeer division of the tribe, considerably hampering their progress. It represents, however, a variety of the older form of stationary house used when the Chukchee were a purely maritime people.[9]

It might be objected that maladjustments of this sort are transitional, that just as the copper and bronze workers ultimately freed themselves from the influence of the preëxisting stone technique so the Chukchee would finally have abandoned their inconvenient tent and developed a new and more readily transportable lodge. This sounds, of course, very plausible but misses the point of the argument. Undoubtedly, a more and more perfect adaptation to elements of the physical surroundings has repeatedly taken place. But the very fact that culture history, on its material side, implies this progressive adjustment also implies that the cultural phenomena at different periods of time differ where the same environmental stimuli persist and therefore cannot be explained by them, which is what we have been trying to prove.

Indeed, environment is not only unable to create cultural features, in some instances it is even incapable of perpetuating them. Thus, pottery was once distributed over an extensive region in the New Hebrides but is now restricted to a few isolated localities on a single island. Again, in southeastern New Guinea ancient pottery has been found that vastly surpasses its present representatives in point of craftsmanship.[10] A similar phenomenon has been noted in the Southwest of the United States, where the evolution and deterioration of glazed earthenware may be clearly traced in the same region.[11] Dr. Rivers has pointed out an even more instructive example of cultural degeneration. In the Torres Islands of Melanesia the natives have no canoes for traversing the channels which separate their islands from one another but are obliged to use unseaworthy bamboo rafts inadequate even for fishing purposes. Yet there is evidence that the Torres Islanders once shared the art of canoe-making with their fellow-Oceanians and that it has died out in recent times independently of European influence. It is difficult to conceive of any people less likely *a priori* to lose the art of navigation than a South Sea Island group; yet, their maritime environment proved inadequate to preserve so vital a feature of their daily life.

To sum up: Environment cannot explain culture because the identical environment is consistent with distinct cultures; because cultural traits persist from inertia in an unfavorable environment; because they do not develop where they would be of distinct advantage to a people; and because they may even disappear where one would least expect it on geographical principles.

Shall we then cavalierly banish geography from cultural considerations? This would be manifestly going beyond the mark. Geographical phenomena can no more be discarded than can psychological phenomena. They represent in the first place a limiting condition. As cultures cannot contravene psychological principles so they cannot, except in a limited measure, override geographical factors. To use some drastically clear if somewhat hackneyed examples, the Eskimo do not eat coconuts nor do the Oceanians build snow-houses; where the horse does not occur it cannot be domesticated; in the Hopi country where watercourses are lacking navigation naturally did not develop. As Jochelson points out, the Koryak of north-eastern Siberia cannot cultivate cereals because of the low temperature and they cannot succeed as cattle-breeders because of the poor quality of the grasses.[12] This minimum recognition of environment as a purely negative factor, however, does not do full justice to it. Take the bison out of the Plains Indian's life and his cultural atmosphere certainly changes. Nevertheless, we have seen that the presence of the bison by no means fully determined the cultural employment possible. Instead of hunting it as the Solutrean Europeans did the wild horse, the Indian might have domesticated it as his namesake by misnomer in Asia domesticated the buffalo. The environment, then, enters into culture, not as a formative but rather as an inert element ready to be selected from and molded. It is, of course, a matter of biological necessity for a people to establish some sort of adaptation to surrounding conditions, but such adaptation is no more spontaneously generated by the environment than are strictly biological adaptations. There are alternatives to adaptation—migration and destruction.

It is true, as Dr. Wissler has forcibly pointed out, that when some kind of adjustment has once been established it will tend to persist in the region of its origin.[13] This, however, illustrates not so much the active influence of environment as rather the tremendous force of cultural inertia which tends to perpetuate an old muddling-along adjustment, however imperfect, provided only it has bare survival value.

Altogether we may illustrate the relations of culture to environment by an analogy used by Dr. Wissler in another connection, which also brings us back to my initial analogy of the environmental theory with the associationist system in psychology. The environment furnishes the builders of cultural structures with brick and mortar but it does not furnish the architect's plan. As the illustrations cited clearly prove, there is a variety of ways in which the same materials can be put together, nay, there is always a range of choice as regards the materials themselves. The development of a particular architectural style and the selection of a special material from among an indefinite number of possible styles and materials are what characterize a given culture. Since geography permits more than a single adjustment to the same conditions, it cannot give the interpretation sought by the student of culture. Culture can no more be built up of environmental blocks than can consciousness out of isolated ideas; and as the association of ideas already implies the synthetizing faculty of consciousness, so the assemblage and use of environmental factors after a definite plan already implies the selective and synthetic agency of a preëxisting or nascent culture.

IV. THE DETERMINANTS OF CULTURE

Psychology, racial differences, geographical environment, have all proved inadequate for the interpretation of cultural phenomena. The inference is obvious. Culture is a thing *sui generis* which can be explained only in terms of itself. This is not mysticism but sound scientific method. The biologist, whatever metaphysical speculations he may indulge in as to the ultimate origin of life, does not depart in his workaday mood from the principle that every cell is derived from some other cell. So the ethnologist will do well to postulate the principle, *Omnis cultura ex cultura.*[1] This means that he will account for a given cultural fact by merging it in a group of cultural facts or by demonstrating some other cultural fact out of which it has developed. The cultural phenomenon to be explained may either have an antecedent within the culture of the tribe where it is found or it may have been imported from without. Both groups of determinants must be considered.

The extraneous determinants of culture summed up under the heading of 'diffusion' or 'contact of peoples' have been repeatedly referred to in the preceding pages. A somewhat detailed examination seems desirable, for it is difficult to exaggerate their importance.

"Civilization," says Tylor, "is a plant much oftener propagated than developed;"[2] and the latest ethnographic memoir that comes to hand voices the same sentiment: "It is and has always been much easier to borrow an idea from one's neighbors than to originate a new idea; and transmission of cultural elements, which in all ages has taken place in a great many different ways, is and has been one of the greatest promoters of cultural development."[3]

A stock illustration of cultural assimilation is that of the Japanese, who in the nineteenth century adopted our scientific and technological civilization ready-made, just as at an earlier period they had acquired wholesale the culture of China. It is essential to note that it is not always the people of lower culture who remain passive recipients in the process of diffusion. This is strikingly shown by the spread of Indian corn. The white colonist "did not simply borrow the maize seed and then in conformity with his already established agricultural methods, or on original lines, develop a maize culture of his own," but "took over the entire material complex of maize culture" as found among the aborigines.[4] The history of Indian corn also illustrates the remarkable rapidity with which cultural possessions may travel over the globe. Unknown in the Old World prior to the discovery of America, it is mentioned as known in Europe in 1539 and had reached China between 1540 and 1570.[5]

The question naturally arises here, whether this process of diffusion, which in modern times is a matter of direct observation, could have been of importance during the earlier periods of human history when means of communication were of a more primitive order. So far as this point is concerned, we must always remember that methods of transportation progressed very slightly from the invention of the wheeled cart until the most recent times. As Montelius suggests, the periods of 1700 B.C. and 1700 A.D. differed far less in this regard than might be supposed on superficial consideration. Yet we know the imperfection of facilities for travel did not prevent dissemination of culture in historic times.

The great Swedish archæologist has, indeed, given us a most fascinating picture of the commercial relations of northern Europe in earlier periods and their effect on cultural development.[6] We learn with astonishment that in the ninth and tenth centuries of our era, trade was carried on with great intensity between the North of Europe and the Mohammedan culture sphere since tens of thousands of Arabic coins have been found on Swedish soil. But intercourse with remote countries dates back to a far greater antiquity. One of the most powerful stimuli of commercial relations between northern and southern Europe was the desire of the more southern populations to secure amber, a material confined to the Baltic region and occurring more particularly about Jutland and the mouth of the Vistula. Amber beads have been found not only in Swiss pile-dwellings[7] but also in Mycenæan graves of the second millennium B. C. Innumerable finds of amber work in Italy and other parts of southern Europe prove the importance attached to this article, which was exchanged for copper and bronze. The composition of Scandinavian bronzes indicates that their material was imported not from England but from the far-away regions of central Europe. That bronze was not of indigenous manufacture is certain because tin does not occur in Sweden at all while the copper deposits of northern Scandinavia remained untouched until about 1500 years after the end of the Bronze Age. Considering the high development of the bronze technique in Scandinavia and the fact that every pound of bronze had to be imported from without, it would be difficult to exaggerate the extent of contact with the southern populations. But intercourse was not limited to the South. For example, Swedish weapons and implements have been discovered in Finland. Again, crescent-shaped gold ornaments of Irish provenance have been found in Denmark, while a Swedish rock-painting represents with painstaking exactness a type of bronze shield common at a certain prehistoric period of England.

Montelius shows that historical connections of the type so amply attested for the Bronze Age also obtained in the preceding Neolithic era. Swedish hammers of stone dating back to the third pre-Christian millennium and flint daggers have been found in Finland, and earthenware characteristic of Neolithic Scandinavia also turns up on the Baltic coast of Russia. Stone burial cists with a peculiar oval opening at one end occur in a limited section of southwestern Sweden and likewise in England. Since such monuments have been discovered neither in other parts of Sweden nor in Jutland or the Danish islands, they point to a direct intercourse between Britain and western Sweden at about

2,000 B.C. A still older form of burial unites Scandinavia with other parts of the continent. Chambers built up of large stones set up edgewise and reaching from the floor to the roof, the more recent ones with and the older without a long covered passage, are highly characteristic of Sweden, Denmark, the British Isles, and the coasts of Europe from the Vistula embouchure to the coasts of France and Portugal, of Italy, Greece, the Crimea, North Africa, Syria, and India. Specific resemblances convince the most competent judges that some, at least, of these widely diffused 'dolmens' are historically connected with their Swedish equivalents, and since the oldest of these Northern chambers go back 3,000 years before our era, we thus have evidence of cultural diffusion dating back approximately five millennia.

It is highly interesting to trace under Montelius' guidance the development of culture as it seems to have actually taken place in southern Sweden. Beginning with the earliest periods, we find the coastal regions inhabited by a population of fishermen and hunters. At a subsequent stage coarse pottery appears with articles of bone and antler, and there is evidence that the dog has become domesticated. In the later Neolithic era perfectly polished stone hammers and exquisitely chipped flint implements occur, together with indications that cattle, horses, sheep and pigs are domesticated and that the cultivation of the soil has begun. Roughly speaking, we may assume that the culture of Scandinavia at the end of the Stone Age resembled in advancement that of the agricultural North American and Polynesian tribes as found by the first European explorers. We may assume a long period of essentially indigenous cultural growth followed towards its close by intimate relations with alien populations. Nevertheless, it was the more extensive contact of the Bronze period that rapidly raised the ancestral Swedes to a cultural position high above a primitive level, with accentuation of agriculture, the use of woolen clothing, and a knowledge of metallurgy. It was again foreign influence that later brought the knowledge of iron and in the third century of our era transformed the Scandinavians into a literary people, flooded their country with art products of the highest then existing Roman civilization, and ultimately introduced Christianity.

The case of Scandinavian culture is fairly typical. We have first a long-continued course of leisurely and relatively undisturbed development, which is superseded by a tremendously rapid assimilation of cultural elements from without. Through contact with tribes possessing a higher civilization the ancient Scandinavians came to participate in its benefits and even to excel in special departments of it, such as bronze work, which from lack of material, they would have been physically incapable of developing unaided. Diffusion was the determinant of Scandinavian cultural progress from savagery to civilization.

It is obvious that this insistence on contact of peoples as a condition of cultural evolution does not solve the ultimate problem of the origin of culture. The question naturally obtrudes itself: If the Scandinavians obtained their civilization from the Southeast, how did the Oriental cultures themselves originate? Nevertheless, when we examine these higher civilizations of the Old World, we are again met with indubitable evidence that one of the conditions of development is the contact of peoples and the consequent diffusion of cultural elements. This appears clearly from a consideration of the ancient civilizations of Egypt, Babylonia, and China.

We now have abundant evidence for a later Stone Age in Egypt with an exceptionally high development of the art of chipping, as well as specimens of pottery and other indications of a sedentary mode of life. About 5,000 B.C. this undisturbed evolution began to suffer from a series of migrations of West Asiatic tribes, bringing in their wake a number of cultivated plants and domesticated animals, as well as various other features which possibly included the art of smelting copper, while the ceramic ware of the earlier period agrees so largely with that of Elam in what is now southern Persia that a cultural connection seems definitely established.

If from Egypt we turn to the most probable source of alien culture elements found there, *viz.*, to the region of Mesopotamia, possibly the oldest seat of higher civilization in Asia, we find again that the culture of Babylonia under the famous lawgiver Hammurabi (about 2,000 B.C.) is not the product of purely indigenous growth but represents the resultant of at least two components, that of the Sumerian civilization of southern Babylonia and the Accadian culture of the North. It is certain that the Accadians adopted the art of writing from the Sumerians and were also stimulated by this contact in their artistic development. The evolution of Sumerian civilization is lost in obscurity but on the basis of well-established historical cases we should hesitate to assign to them an exclusively creative, and to other populations an exclusively receptive, rôle.

We may quite safely assume that the early splendor of Sumerian civilization was also in large part due to stimuli received through foreign relations. That cultural elements of value may be borrowed from an inferior as well as from a higher level, has already been exemplified by the case of maize. It is also, among other things, illustrated by the history of the Chinese.

The Chinese have generally been represented as developing in complete isolation from other peoples. This traditional conception, however, breaks down with more intimate knowledge. Dr. Laufer has demonstrated that Chinese civilization, too, is a complex structure due to the conflux of distinct cultural streams. As an originally inland people inhabiting the middle and lower course of the Yellow River, they gradually reached the coast and acquired the art of navigation through contact with Indo-Chinese seafarers. Acquaintance with the northern nomads of Turkish and Tungus stock led to the use of the horse, donkey and camel, as well as the practice of felt and rug weaving, possibly even to the adoption of furniture and the iron technique.[8] Most important of all, it appears that essentials of agriculture, cattle-raising, metallurgy and pottery, as well as less tangible features of civilization are common to ancient China and Babylonia, which forces us to the conclusion that both the Chinese and Babylonian cultures are ramifications from a common Asiatic sub-stratum. It would be idle to speculate as to the relative contributions of each center to this ancient cultural stock. The essential point is that the most ancient Asiatic civilizations of which we have any evidence already indicate close contact of peoples and the dispersal of cultural elements.

Contact of peoples is thus an extraordinary promoter of cultural development. By the free exchange of arts and ideas among a group of formerly independent peoples, a superiority and complexity is rendered possible which without such diffusion would never have occurred. The part played in this process by the cruder populations must not be underestimated. They may contribute both actively and passively; actively, by transmitting knowledge independently acquired, as in the case of the felt technique the Chinese learned from the northern nomads; passively, by forming a lower caste on which the economic labors devolve and thus liberating their conquerors for an enlarged activity in the less utilitarian spheres of culture.

Nevertheless, before peoples can communicate their cultures to others with whom they come into contact, they must first evolve these cultures.

The question thus remains, What determines this evolution? In order to gain a proper perspective in this matter, we must for a moment consider the progress of human civilization as a whole. Archæological research shows that the modern era of steel and iron tools was preceded by an age of bronze and copper implements, which in turn was preceded by a stone age subdivided into a more recent period of polished, and an earlier of merely chipped, stone tools. Now the chronological relations of these epochs are extremely suggestive. The very lowest estimate by any competent observer of the age of Palæolithic man in Europe sets it at 50,000 years;[9] since this is avowedly the utmost minimum value that can be assigned on geological grounds, we may reasonably assume twice that figure for the age of human culture generally. Using the rough estimate permissible in discussions of this sort, we may regard the end of the Palæolithic era as dating back about 15,000 years ago. In short, for more than eight-tenths of its existence, the human species remained at a cultural level at best comparable with that of the Australian. We may assume that it was during this immense space of time that dispersal over the face of the globe took place and that isolation fixed the broader diversities of language and culture, over and above what may have been the persisting cultural sub-stratum common to the earliest undivided human group. The following Neolithic period of different parts of the globe terminated at different times and had not been passed at all by most of the American aborigines and the Oceanians at the time of their discovery. However, from the broader point of view here assumed, it was not relieved by the age of metallurgy until an exceedingly recent past. The earliest estimate I have seen does not put the event back farther than 6000 B.C. even in Mesopotamia. During nine-tenths of his existence, then, man was ignorant of the art of smelting copper from the ore. Finally, the iron technique does not date back 4,000 years; it took humanity ninety-six hundredths of its existence to develop this art.

We may liken the progress of mankind to that of a man a hundred years old, who dawdles through kindergarten for eighty-five years of his life, takes ten years to go through .the primary grades, then rushes with lightning rapidity through grammar school, high school and college. Culture, it seems, is a matter of exceedingly slow growth until a certain 'threshold' is passed, when it darts forward, gathering momentum at an unexpected rate. For this peculiarity of culture as a whole, many miniature parallels exist in special subdivisions of culture history. Natural science lay dormant until Kepler, Galileo and Newton stirred it into unexampled activity, and the same holds for applied science until about a century ago.

This discontinuity of development receives strong additional illustration from a survey of special subdivisions of ancient culture. Though the Palæolithic era certainly preceded the later Stone Age, archæologists have hitherto failed to show the steps by which the later could develop out of the earlier. This gap may, of course, be due merely to our lack of knowledge. Yet when we take subdivisions of the Palæolithic period, the same fact once more confronts us. There is no orderly progression from Solutrean to Magdalenian times. The highly developed flint technique of the former dwindles away in the latter and its place is taken by what seems a spontaneous generation of bone and ivory work, with a high development of realistic art.

In view of the evidence, it seems perfect nonsense to say that early European civilization, by some law inherent in the very nature of culture, developed in the way indicated by archæological finds. Southern Scandinavia could not possibly have had a bronze age without alien influence.

In this case, discontinuity was the result of cultural contact. It may be that the lack of definite direction observed throughout the Stone Age may in part be due to similar causes, the migrations and contact of different peoples, as Professor Sollas suggests. But it is important to note that discontinuity is a necessary feature of cultural progress. It does not matter whether we can determine the particular point in the series at which the significant trait was introduced. It does not matter whether, as I have suggested in the discussion of racial features, the underlying *causes* of the phenomena proceed with perfect continuity. Somewhere in the observed cultural *effects* there is the momentous innovation that leads to a definite break with the past. From a broad point of view, for example, it is immaterial whether the doctrine of evolution clings to the name of the younger or the elder Darwin, to Lamarck or St. Hilaire; the essential thing is that somehow the idea originated, and that when it had taken root it produced incalculable results in modern thought.

If culture, even when uninfluenced by foreign contact, progresses by leaps and bounds, we should naturally like to ascertain the determinants of such 'mutations.' In this respect, the discontinuity of indigenous evolution differs somewhat from that connected with cultural development due to diffusion. It was absolutely impossible that Scandinavia should produce bronze in the absence of tin. But *a priori* it is conceivable that an undisturbed culture might necessarily develop by what biologists call 'orthogenetic evolution', *i.e.*, in a definite direction through definite stages. This is, indeed, what is commonly known as the classical scheme of cultural evolution, of which men like Morgan are the protagonists. Now, how do the observed facts square with this theoretical possibility?

As Professor Boas and American ethnologists generally have maintained,[10] many facts are quite inconsistent with the theory of unilinear evolution. That theory can be tested very simply by comparing the sequence of events in two or more areas in which independent development has taken place. For example, has technology in Africa followed the lines ascertained for ancient Europe? We know today that it has not. Though unlike southern Scandinavia, the Dark Continent is not lacking in copper deposits, the African Stone Age was not superseded by a Copper Age, but directly by a period of Iron. Similarly, I have already pointed out that the possession of the same domesticated animals does not produce the same economic utilization of them while the Tungus rides his reindeer, other Siberians harness their animals to a sledge; the Chinaman will not milk his cattle, while the Zulu's diet consists largely of milk. That a particular innovation occurred at a given time and place is, of course, no less the result of definite causes than any other phenomenon of the universe. But often it seems to have been caused by an accidental complex of conditions rather than in accordance with some fixed principle.

For example, the invention of the wheel revolutionized methods of transportation. Now, why did this idea develop in the Old World and never take root among the American Indians? We are here face to face with one of those ultimate data that must simply be accepted like the physicist's fact that water expands in freezing while other substances contract. So far as we can see, the invention might have been made in America as well as not; and for all we know it would never have been made there until the end of time. This introduces a very important consideration. A given culture is, in a measure, at least, a unique phenomenon. In so far as this is true it must defy generalized treatment, and the explanation of a cultural phenomenon will consist in referring it back to the particular circumstances that preceded it. In other words, the explanation will consist in a recital of its past history; or, to put it negatively, it cannot involve the assumption of an organic law of cultural evolution that would necessarily produce the observed effect.

Facts already cited in other connections may be quoted again by way of illustration. When a copper implement is fashioned not according to the requirements of the material, but in direct imitation of preëxisting stone patterns, we have an instance of cultural inertia: it is only the past history of technology that renders the phenomena conceivable. So the unwieldy Chukchee tent, which adheres to the style of a pre-nomadic existence, is explained as soon as the past history of the tribe comes to light.

Phenomena that persist in isolation from their original context are technically known as 'survivals', and form one of the most interesting chapters of ethnology. One or two additional examples will render their nature still clearer. The boats of the Vikings were equipped for rowing as well as for sailing. Why the superfluous appliances for rowing, which were later dropped? As soon as we learn that the Norse boats were originally rowboats and that sails were a later addition, the rowing equipment is placed in its proper cultural setting and the problem is solved. Another example may be offered from a different phase of life. Among the Arapaho Indians there is a series of dance organizations graded by age. Membership is acquired by age-mates at the same time, each receiving the requisite ceremonial instructions from some older man who passed through the dance in his day. These older men, who are paid for their services by the candidates, may belong to any and all of the higher organizations. Oddly enough, each group of dancers is assisted by a number of 'elder brothers', all of whom rank them by *two* grades in the series of dancers. This feature is not at all clear from the Arapaho data alone. When, however, we turn to the Hidatsa Indians, with whom there is evidence this system of age-societies originated, we find that here the youngest group of men does not buy instructions from a miscellaneous assemblage of older men, but buys the dance outright from the whole of the second grade; this group, in order to have the privilege of performing a dance, must buy that of the third grade, and so on. In all these purchases the selling group seeks to extort the highest possible price while the buyers try to get off as cheaply as possible and are aided by the second higher group, *i.e.*, the group just ranking the sellers. Here the sophomore-senior versus freshman-junior relationship is perfectly intelligible; both the freshman and the junior, to pursue the analogy, bear a natural economic hostility against the sophomore, and vice versa. The Arapaho usage is intelligible as a survival from this earlier Hidatsa condition.

Our own civilization is shot through with survivals, so that further illustrations are unnecessary. They suggest, however, another aspect of our general problem. Of course, in every culture different traits are linked together without there being any essential bond between them. An illustration of this type of association is that mentioned by Dr. Laufer for Asiatic tribes, *viz.*, that all nations which use milk for their diet have epic poems, while those which abstain from milk have no epic literature. This type of chance association, due to historical causes, has been discussed by Dr. Wissler[11] and Professor Czekanowski.[12] But survivals show that there may be an *organic* relation between phenomena that have become separated and are treated as distinct by the descriptive ethnologist. In such cases, one trait is the determinant of the other, possibly as the actually preceding cause, possibly as part of the same phenomenon in the sense in which the side of a triangle is correlated with an angle.

A pair of illustrations will elucidate the matter. Primitive terms of relationship often reveal characteristic differences of connotation from their nearest equivalents in European languages. On the other hand, they are remarkably similar not only among many of the North American Indians but also in many other regions of the globe, such as Australia, Oceanica, Africa. The most striking peculiarity of this system of nomenclature lies in the inclusiveness of certain terms. For example, the word we translate as 'father' is applied indiscriminately to the father, all his brothers, and some of his male cousins; while the word for 'mother' is correspondingly used for the mother's sisters and some of their female cousins. On the other hand, paternal and maternal uncle or aunt are rigidly distinguished by a difference in terminology. As Morgan divined and Tylor clearly recognized, this system is connected with the one-sided exogamous kin organization by which an individual is reckoned as belonging to the exogamous social group of one, and only one, of his parents. The terminology that appears so curious at first blush then resolves itself very simply into the method of calling those members of the tribe who belong to the father's social group and generation by the same term as the father, while the maternal uncles, who must belong to another group because of the exogamous rule, are distinguished from the father. In short, the terminology simply expresses the existing social organization. In a world-wide survey of the field Tylor found that the number of peoples who use the type of nomenclature I have described and are divided into exogamous groups, is about three times that to be expected on the doctrine of chances: in other words, the two apparently distinct phenomena are causally connected.[13] This interpretation has recently been forcibly advocated by Dr. Rivers, and I have examined the North American data from this point of view. It developed, as a matter of fact, that practically all the tribes with exogamous 'clans', *i.e.*, matrilineal kin groups, or exogamous 'gentes', *i.e.*, patrilineal kin groups, had a system of the type described, while most of the tribes lacking such groups also lacked the nomenclature in question. Accordingly, it follows that there is certainly a functional relation between these phenomena, although it is conceivable that both are functionally related to still other phenomena, and that the really significant relationship remains to be determined.

As a linked illustration, the following phenomena may be presented. Among the Crow of Montana, the Hopi of Arizona, and some Melanesian tribes, the same term is applied to a father's sister and to a father's sister's daughter;

indeed, among the Crow and the Hopi the term is extended to all the female descendants through females of the father's sister *ad infinitum*. Such a usage is at once intelligible from the tendency to call females of the father's group belonging to his and younger generations by a single term, regardless of generation, *if* descent is reckoned through the mother, for in that case, and that case only, will the individuals in question belong to the same group. And the fact is that in each of the cases mentioned, group affiliation is traced through the mother, while I know of not a single instance in which paternal descent coexists with the nomenclatorial disregard of generations in the form described.

My instances show, then, that cultural traits may be functionally related, and this fact renders possible a parallelism, however limited, of cultural development in different parts of the globe. The field of culture, then, is not a region of complete lawlessness. Like causes produce like effects here as elsewhere, though the complex conditions with which we are grappling require unusual caution in definitely correlating phenomena. It is true that American ethnologists have shown that in several instances like phenomena can be traced to diverse causes; that, in short, unlike antecedents converge to the same point.

However, at the risk of being anathematized as a person of utterly unhistorical mentality, I must register my belief that this point has been overdone and that the continued insistence on it by Americanists is itself an illustration of cultural inertia. Indeed, the vast majority of so-called convergencies are not genuine, but false analogies due to our throwing together diverse facts from ignorance of their true nature, just as an untutored mind will class bats with birds, or whales with fish. When, however, rather full knowledge reveals not superficial resemblance but absolute identity of cultural features, it would be miraculous, indeed, to assume that such equivalence somehow was shaped by different determinants. When a Zulu of South Africa, an Australian, and a Crow Indian all share the mother-in-law taboo imposing mutual avoidance on the wife's mother and the daughter's husband, with exactly the same psychological correlate, it is, to my mind, rash to decree without attempt to produce evidence that this custom must, in each case, have developed from entirely distinct motives. To be sure, this particular usage has not yet, in my opinion, been satisfactorily accounted for. Nevertheless, in contradistinction to some of my colleagues and to the position I myself once shared, I now believe that it is pusillanimous to shirk the real problem involved, and that in so far as any explanation admits the problem, any explanation is preferable to the flaunting of fine phrases about the unique character of cultural phenomena. When, however, we ask what sort of explanation could be given, we find that it is by necessity a *cultural* explanation. Tylor, *e.g.*, thinks that the custom is correlated with the social rule that the husband takes up his abode with the wife's relatives and that the taboo merely marks the difference between him and the rest of the family. We have here clearly one cultural phenomenon as the determinant of another.

It is not so difficult as might at first appear to harmonize the principle that a cultural phenomenon is explicable only by a unique combination of antecedent circumstances with the principle that like phenomena are the product of like antecedents. The essential point is that in either case we have past history as the determinant. It is not necessary that certain things should happen; but if they do happen, then there is at least a considerable likelihood that certain other things will also happen. Diversity occurs where the particular thing of importance, say the wheel, has been discovered or conceived in one region but not in another. Parallelism tends to occur when the same significant phenomenon is shared by distinct cultures. It remains true that in culture history we are generally wise after the event. *A priori*, who would not expect that milking must follow from the domestication of cattle?

When we find that a type of kinship terminology is determined by exogamy or matrilineal descent, we have, indeed, given a cultural explanation of a cultural fact; but for the ultimate problems how exogamy or maternal descent came about, we may be unable to give a solution. Very often we cannot ascertain an anterior or correlated cultural fact for another cultural fact, but can merely group it with others of the same kind. Of this order are many of the parallels that figure so prominently in ethnological literature. For example, that primitive man everywhere believes in the animation of nature seems an irreducible datum which we can, indeed, paraphrase and turn hither and thither for clearer scrutiny but can hardly reduce to simpler terms. All we can do is to merge any particular example of such animism in the general class after the fashion of all scientific interpretation. That certain tendencies of all but universal occurrence are characteristic of culture, no fair observer can deny, and it is the manifest business of ethnology to ascertain all such regularities so that as many cultural phenomena as possible may fall into their appropriate categories. Only those who would derive each and every trait similar in different communities of human beings from a single geographical source can ignore such general characteristics of culture, which may, in a sense, be regarded as determinants of specific cultural data or rather, as the principles of which these are particular manifestations.

Recently I completed an investigation of Plains Indian societies begun on the most rigorous of historical principles, with a distinct bias in favor of the unique character of cultural data. But after smiting hip and thigh the assumption that the North American societies were akin to analogous institutions in Africa and elsewhere, I came face to face with the fact that, after all, among the Plains Indians, as among other tribes, the tendency of age-mates to flock together had formed social organizations and thus acted as a cultural determinant.

Beyond such interpretative principles for special phases of civilization, there are still broader generalizations of cultural phenomena. One has been repeatedly alluded to under the caption of cultural inertia, or survival—the irrational persistence of a feature when the context in which it had a place has vanished. But culture is not merely a passive phenomenon but a dynamic one as well. This is strikingly illustrated in the assimilation of an alien cultural stimulus. As I have already pointed out, it is not sufficient to bring two cultures into contact in order to have a perfect cultural interpenetration. The element of selection enters in a significant way. Not everything that is offered by a foreign culture is borrowed. The Japanese have accepted our technology but not our religion and etiquette. Moreover, what is accepted may undergo a very considerable change. While the whole range of phenomena is extremely wide and cannot be dismissed with a few words, it appears fairly clear that generally the preëxisting culture at once seizes upon a foreign element and models it in accordance with the *native* pattern. Thus, the Crow Indians, who had had a pair of rival organizations, borrowed a society from the Hidatsa where such rivalry did not exist. Straightway, the Crow imposed on the new society their own conception, and it became the competitor of another of their organizations. Similarly the Pawnee have a highly developed star cult. Their folklore is in many regards similar to that of other Plains tribes, from which some tales have undoubtedly been borrowed.

Yet in the borrowing these stories became changed and the same episodes which elsewhere relate to human heroes now receive an astral setting. The preëxisting cultural pattern synthetizes the new element with its own preconceptions.

Another tendency that is highly characteristic of all cultures is the rationalistic explanation of what reason never gave rise to. This is shown very clearly in the justification of existing cultural features or of opinions acquired as a member of a particular society. Hegel's notion that whatever exists is rational and Pope's 'whatever is, is right' have their parallels in primitive legend and the literature of religious and political partisanship. In the special form of justification employed we find again the determining influence of the surrounding cultural atmosphere. Among the Plains Indians almost everything is explained as the result of supernatural revelation; if a warrior has escaped injury in battle it is because he wore a feather bestowed on him in a vision; if he acquires a large herd of horses it is in fulfilment of a spiritistic communication during the fast of adolescence. In a community where explanations of this type hold sway, we are not surprised to find that the origin of rites, too, is almost uniformly traced to a vision and that even the most trivial alteration in ceremonial garb is not claimed as an original invention but ascribed to supernatural promptings. Thus, the existing culture acts doubly as the determinant of the explanation offered for a particular cultural phenomenon. It evokes the search for its own *raison d'être;* and the type of interpretation called forth conforms to the explanatory pattern characteristic of the culture involved.

Culture thus appears as a closed system. We may not be able to explain all cultural phenomena or at least not beyond a certain point; but inasmuch as we *can* explain them at all, explanation must remain on the cultural plane.

What are the determinants of culture? We have found that cultural traits may be transmitted from without and in so far forth are determined by the culture of an alien people. The extraordinary extent to which such diffusion has taken place proves that the actual development of a given culture does not conform to innate laws necessarily leading to definite results, such hypothetical laws being overridden by contact with foreign peoples. But even where a culture is of relatively indigenous growth comparison with other cultures suggests that one step does not necessarily lead to another, that an invention like the wheel or the domestication of an animal occurs in one place and does not occur in another. To the extent of such diversity we must abandon the quest for general formulæ of cultural evolution and recognize as the determinant of a phenomenon the unique course of its past history. However, there is not merely discontinuity and diversity but also stability and agreement in the sphere of culture. The discrete steps that mark culture history may not determine one another, but each may involve as a necessary or at least probable consequence other phenomena which in many instances are simply new aspects of the same phenomenon, and in so far forth one cultural element as isolated in description is the determinant or correlate of another. As for those phenomena which we are obliged to accept as realities without the possibility of further analysis, we can, at least, classify a great number of them and merge particular instances in a group of similar facts. Finally, there are dominant characteristics of culture, like cultural inertia or the secondary rationalization of habits acquired irrationally by the members of a group, which serve as broad interpretative principles in the history of civilization.

In short, as in other sciences, so in ethnology there are ultimate, irreducible facts, special functional relations, and principles of wider scope that guide us through the chaotic maze of detail. And as the engineer calls on the physicist for a knowledge of mechanical laws, so the social builder of the future who should seek to refashion the culture of his time and add to its cultural values will seek guidance from ethnology, the science of culture, which in Tylor's judgment is 'essentially a reformer's science.'

V. TERMS OF RELATIONSHIP

Most descriptive monographs on primitive tribes contain lists of the words with which the natives designate their relatives by blood and marriage. The reason is far from obvious. Why should not this topic be left in the hands of a linguist-lexicographer? It is true that primitive usage in this regard is very quaint from our point of view, but so are primitive conceptions on a variety of subjects that likewise find expression in speech. The refinement of spatial distinctions in North American languages, the classification of colors or animals or other groups of natural phenomena are of equal intrinsic interest from a psychological point of view. Why, then, single out a particular department of the aboriginal vocabulary in a treatise on culture? The answer is simply this, that kinship terms have a direct relation to cultural data.

The very fact that primitive tribes frequently use terms of kinship as words of address where we should substitute personal names is a social practice of ethnological interest. But the essential point is that the terms used are often very definitely correlated with specific social usages. Generally speaking, the use of distinct words for two types of relatives is connected with a real difference in their social relations to the speaker. Thus, a majority of primitive tribes draw no distinction between the father's sister's daughter and the mother's brother's daughter. But among the Miwok of California, where one of the cousins may be married while the other is within the prohibited degrees, a discrimination is made in language. Again, in many regions of the globe an altogether special bond connects the maternal uncle with the sister's son, and accordingly we find that he is very often sharply distinguished from the paternal uncle in nomenclature.

On the other hand, we can often explain very naturally the use of a single word for two or more relatives whom we designate by as many distinct words. The Vedda of Ceylon, for example, call the man's father-in-law and maternal uncle by the same term. The reason is that here a man commonly marries his mother's brother's daughter; the mother's brother *is* his father-in-law, and this identity is expressed in the terminology. A different illustration is supplied by the Crow of Montana, who have one term for the man's mother-in-law and his wife's brother's wife. The simple explanation is that both stand to him in the relationship of mutual avoidance, and it is this social fact that is expressed by the common designation. The same Indians apply the word for 'father' in a very inclusive manner, possibly to dozens of individuals; but closer examination shows that all of the people so addressed are entitled to the same kind of treatment by the speaker, to a peculiar form of reverence, and to a preferential rank in the distribution of gifts.

These few and casual examples possibly suffice to show why kinship terms deserve the ethnologist's attention. Terms of relationship are, in some measure, indices of social usage. Where relatives whom other people distinguish are grouped together, there is some likelihood that the natives regard them as representing the same relationship because they actually enjoy the same privileges or exercise the same functions in tribal life. Where relatives whom other peoples group together are distinguished, there is some probability that the distinction goes hand in hand with a difference in social function.

Lewis H. Morgan, the pioneer in this domain of knowledge, was keenly alive to the social implications of kinship nomenclature. But while he endeavored to give an ultimate interpretation of it in terms of various social conditions, he was confronted with the fact that not every tribe had a terminology *sui generis*, but that nomenclatures of remote peoples were sometimes marvelously similar. Morgan boldly argued that such community of nomenclature established ultimate racial unity and on this ground coolly suggested a racial connection between the Hawaiians and the South African Zulu, between the natives of India and those of the Western Hemisphere.[1]

These speculations as to racial affinity have been rightly disregarded by later students, because to accept Morgan's premises means running counter to the most obvious facts of physical anthropology. As Lubbock pointed out, we cannot assume that the Two-Mountain Iroquois are more closely akin to remote Oceanians than to their fellow Iroquois because some of their kinship terms resemble in connotation those of the Hawaiians. Nevertheless, Morgan was right in feeling that *some* historical conclusions could be drawn from similarities of relationship nomenclature. We must simply bring this particular group of ethnological data under the same principle as other cultural phenomena. When the same feature occurs within a definite continuous region, we shall assume that it has developed in a single center and spread by borrowing to other parts of the area. When the same feature occurs in disconnected regions, we shall incline to the theory of independent development and shall inquire whether the course of evolution may have been due to the same cultural determinants, *i.e.*, in this case, to the same social institutions.

After these preliminary remarks, we may turn to a closer scrutiny of the facts.

'Systems'. Abstractly considered, it is conceivable that every individual relative might be designated by a different term of relationship by every other individual, just as each object in nature might theoretically be defined by some distinctive word instead of being placed in some such category as 'tree', 'animal', or 'book'. Indeed, primitive people go rather far in their distinctions. Thus, in the Menomini family circle boys are not called 'son' or 'brother', but each is addressed by a word indicating the order of his birth, the oldest being 'mudjikiwis', the second 'osememau', the third 'akotcosememau', the fourth 'nanaweo'.[2] But in this, as in every other department of language, economy has been exercised and instead of a chaotic number of distinct terms for every possible relationship, there is always a limited series, many distinct individual relationships being always grouped together under a single head. Thus, in English we apply the word 'brother' to a number of individuals regardless of their age relatively to ourselves or to one another and irrespective of the sex of the

speaker. Yet, as the Menomini instance shows, the age distinction might very well have been expressed in speech and there are many Indian languages in which one set of terms is used by female and another by male speakers.

All the terms used by a people to designate their relatives by blood or marriage are jointly called their 'kinship system'. This phrase is wholly misleading, if it is understood to imply that all the constituent elements form a well-articulated whole, for this probably never applies to more than a limited number of them, as will appear presently. But as a convenient word for the entire nomenclature of relationship found in a particular region the word 'system' may be provisionally retained. We may say, then, that systems of different peoples vary in their mode of classifying kin and it seems the ethnographer's first duty to determine the types of system found and their geographical distribution.

At the present moment a satisfactory grouping of the world's kinship systems is impossible, owing to our lack of knowledge of many areas. The task is also rendered very difficult by the frequent coexistence of distinct and even contradictory principles in the same 'system'. Each of these may be defined separately, but to weld both or all of them into a unified whole defies our efforts. For example, the Masai of East Africa, in referring to the paternal uncle, simply combine the stems for 'father', *baba*, and 'brother', *alasche*, thus forming by juxtaposition of these primary terms the compound expression *ol alasche le baba*, which means literally 'the brother of the father'. This mode of defining a relative's status by combining primary terms of relationship or a primary term with a qualifying adjective as in our 'grandfather', is technically known as 'descriptive', and ethnologists are wont to speak of descriptive systems. As a matter of fact, this descriptive principle is highly characteristic of the Masai—but not when relatives are directly addressed by them. In such vocative usage, as it may be called, the father's brother is called *baba* like the father himself; the mother's brother is not designated by a phrase composed of primary stems but by a new stem, *abula*, which is also used reciprocally for the nephew; while *koko* serves to call both a paternal and a maternal aunt. These connotations introduce into the Masai 'system' a discordant principle by which relatives, instead of being defined descriptively, are grouped together in classes. But this 'classificatory' feature by no means characterizes all the vocative nomenclature. By far the majority of relatives are addressed by terms suggestive of the presents of live stock presented to them by the speaker; if the gift consisted of a bull, the word used is *b-ainoni*, from *oinoni*, bull; if an ass was given away, the vocative term is *ba-sigiria*, from *sigiria*, ass; and so forth. Accordingly, the vocative terms cited above are only employed by children, who have not yet presented stock to their kin.[3] In short, Masai terminology is molded by at least three entirely disparate principles.

We shall, accordingly, do well to amend our phraseology and to speak rather of kinship categories, features, or principles of classification than of types of kinship systems.

The Descriptive Principle. When we approach our subject in a purely empirical way, we are confronted with the fact that features do not, as a rule, occur sporadically but are distributed over continuous areas. Imperfect as is our knowledge of African systems, for example, we know that the descriptive feature of the Masai nomenclature does not appear everywhere, but flourishes especially among East African tribes, such as the Shilluk, Dinka, and other Upper Nile populations, and perhaps more widely where Arabic influence extends, the Arabian terminology being of a markedly descriptive character. In East Africa, indeed, there is almost quantitative proof of the dependence of kinship terminology on historical connection and geographical proximity. Among the Baganda, as among most Bantu Negroes, the descriptive feature is lacking and such a relative as the mother's brother's son, instead of being designated by a compound expression, is classed with the brother.[4] The Masai, who live surrounded by Bantu tribes, have a purely descriptive system for non-vocative usage but their vocative forms are in part classificatory, while some neighboring Bantu peoples have a correspondingly mixed system. The Shilluk and Dinka seem to use the descriptive principle exclusively, as do the Arabs. The Masai are undoubtedly closely allied with the Nilotes and markedly different from the Bantu. The conclusion is, therefore, inevitable that their terminology—whatever may be its ultimate *raison d'être*—is a function of their historical relations. They have descriptive features because they belong to a group of peoples of whom such features are characteristic. They have classificatory features because they have come into contact with peoples whose systems were characterized by such features and from whom they have borrowed them. The Shilluk lack the classificatory principle because they have not had the same alien influences as the Masai. The restriction of descriptive features to a definite part of Africa and their amalgamation with other features in the marginal section of this area show that kinship nomenclatures follow precisely the same rules as other elements of culture and that their distribution indicates probable or corroborates known tribal relations.

The descriptive principle is not restricted to East Africa and the Semitic family, but has been found in the Persian, Armenian, Celtic, Esthonian, and Scandinavian languages.[5] Although guesses might be offered, I do not feel that our present knowledge permits definite statements as to the historical relations suggested by the total range of the descriptive principle on the face of the globe.

The Hawaiian Principle. While the term 'descriptive' admits of a fairly unambiguous definition, the same cannot be said for the word 'classificatory'. Morgan, after explaining his use of the former, states that a system of the second type reduces blood-relatives to great classes by a series of apparently arbitrary generalizations, applying the same terms to all the members of the same class. "It thus confounds relationships, which, under the descriptive system, are distinct, and enlarges the signification both of the primary and secondary terms beyond their seemingly appropriate sense."[6] This is looking at the matter from the arbitrarily selected point of view of our own nomenclature (which Morgan improperly, as Rivers has shown, regarded as descriptive). Objectively considered, even descriptive terminologies are classificatory, inasmuch as they do not individualize, but content themselves with such generalizations as classing together, say, all the father's brothers instead of uniformly specializing according to age. For this reason I regard as misplaced Dr. Rivers' emphasis on whether a term designates a single individual or a wider group. What, then, lies at the basis of the classificatory principle? Dr. Rivers, following Tylor, reduces it to the clan factor or rather to the influence of the dual organization of ancient society, by which it was divided into exogamous moieties. But this important suggestion, to which we shall have to revert, applies avowedly only to one form of the classificatory system and involves, therefore, the hypothesis that this preceded other forms. This may prove to be valid, but we cannot prejudice an empirical survey by taking its proof for granted and cannot, therefore, simply substitute 'clan' for 'classificatory' systems—apart from the fact that to talk of systems instead of principles or features in this connection is demonstrably misleading.

It is quite clear that 'classificatory' can be used only in a loose sense, to indicate wider groupings of kin than those to which we are accustomed; and that there is no *necessary* evolutionary relation between the two forms usually classed under this head. The empirical data are simply these. In certain systems, blood-relatives are classed according to generation regardless of nearness of kinship and of their maternal or paternal affiliations; in others, there is bifurcation, the maternal and paternal kin of at least the generations nearest to the speaker being distinguished. We may call the former the 'unforked merging', or geographically the 'Hawaiian' mode of classification; the latter may be correspondingly referred to as 'forked merging', or 'Dakota'. One point which it is essential to remember even at this early stage of our survey is that these principles, together with the descriptive one, are very far from exhausting the varieties found.

Let us now consider the 'unforked' principle somewhat more closely as it finds expression among the Hawaiians. These people apply a single term, *makua*, to both parents and to all their parents' brothers and sisters, sex being distinguished only by qualifying words meaning 'man' and 'woman'. All related individuals of one's generation are classed as brothers and sisters, certain distinctions being drawn according to the age of their parents relatively to that of one's own parents and also according to the speaker's sex, but none resulting from the differences in *nearness* of kinship. The children of all these brothers and sisters are classed with one's own children, and *their* children with one's grandchildren, while a single term embraces grandparents and all related members of their generation.[7] This age-stratification of blood-relatives with disregard of differences as to father's or mother's side occurs not only in Hawaii, but also in New Zealand, Kusaie, the Gilbert and Marshall Islands.[8] It is not uninteresting to note that Hawaii and New Zealand, though far removed from each other, coincide closely in other cultural features not shared with fellow-Polynesians, as Professor Dixon has recently shown in his treatment of Oceanian mythology. The geographical proximity of Micronesia to Hawaii hardly requires mention. Dr. Rivers points out[9] that certain Polynesian tribes in contact with Melanesians, whose systems display essentially the forked principle, *e.g.*, the Tongans, use an intermediate nomenclature. We are thus again able to summarize the data in terms of historical connection. The assumption may be made that the ancient Polynesian terminology was that of

Hawaii and New Zealand, which was modified where the Polynesians came into contact with diverse populations, and is shared by populations whose territory was presumably traversed by the Hawaiians. Dr. Rivers also states that the Burmese, Karen, Chinese and Japanese systems conform to the Hawaiian principle. He seems to depend on Morgan's statement of the case, which may require revision. But, accepting the data as given and assuming that the Malay proper classify kin according to the unforked method, we should still have a perfectly continuous distribution for the Hawaiian features.

This would no longer hold if we accepted Morgan's view that the Zulu of South Africa share the Hawaiian form, on which slender basis he advances the hypothesis that Kaffir and Polynesian have a common ancestry.[10] As a matter of fact, the Zulu nomenclature secured by Morgan does in some instances slur over the difference of paternal and maternal lines, to the exclusive dominance of the generation factor. Thus, man and woman call all the brother's and sister's children their sons and daughters without distinction, and the children of the father's sister are classed with one's brothers and sisters.

Nevertheless, even Morgan's list reveals fundamental deviations from the Hawaiian principle.

As he notes, the mother's brother is *not* classed with the father's brother and father, and the assumption that he formerly was is mere guess-work. What particularly astonished Morgan, however, was that the father's sister was not called mother, but father. This is, indeed, amazing, if we start from our own notions as to the necessity of distinguishing parental sex, and in addition assume that the Zulu system is a variant of the Hawaiian one. If we free our minds from these preconceptions, there is no mystery; the father's sister is classed with the father simply in order to express the difference from the maternal line in accordance with the principle of bifurcation.

In order to gain greater clearness in this matter it is necessary to extend our investigation to other Bantu tribes, preferably to those whose territories approach that of the Zulu. The essential point to ascertain is whether paternal and maternal uncles and aunts are merged in one group or are distinguished.[11] Among the Thonga, who live north of the Zulu, the father's sister, as in Zulu, is classed with the father, the word meaning literally 'female father' and thus emphasizing her separation from the mother's side of the family. The Herero, according to Schinz, seem to class all aunts with the mother in vocative usage, but when not directly referring to these relatives they employ quite distinct expressions for the father's and the mother's sisters. In Baganda the difference between the two sides is marked. *Mange* is mother, and the same word with the qualifier *muto* means mother's sister, while father's sister is *sengawe*. Even clearer is the case for the maternal uncle. In the Ronga group of the Thonga he is called by a distinct word, *malume*, which almost coincides with Morgan's Zulu term. In the Djonga division he is classed with the grandfather, not the father. By a quite distinct stem, the Herero sharply distinguish the mother's brother from the father and his brothers. The same applies to the Baganda. As for the correlative term, from which Morgan infers that the Zulu once called the maternal uncle 'father', the Ronga have a distinct word for nephew, *mupsyana*, while the Djonga who class the mother's brother with the grandfather consistently enough call the sister's son 'grandson'. Among the Herero, though uncles and aunts generally regard their nephews and nieces as their own children, the maternal uncle applies to them a distinct term, *ovasia*. Among the Baganda a man calls his son *mutabani* or *mwana*, but his sister's son is *mujwa*. I may add that the altogether peculiar bond of familiarity that links together mother's brother and sister's son[12] among some Bantu people is inconsistent with Morgan's assumption that the relationships of maternal uncle and father were once grouped under a single head among tribes of this family, for as stated above, such specific social relationships are generally expressed by specific terms for the relatives.

The conditions obtaining within the speaker's generation at first seem to lend some support to the conception of the Bantu system as dominated by the Hawaiian principle, since the terms for brother and sister are more widely employed by some Bantu than is compatible with the forked division of kin. But closer inspection proves that, whatever may be at the root of the Bantu classification, it is not the Hawaiian notion of marking off generations. Even in Morgan's Zulu series, while a man calls his maternal uncle's children by a special term, they address him as brother; that is to say, members of the same generation and sex are not all classed together. Among the Herero, where the children of a brother and sister (but not of *Geschwister* of the same sex) regularly intermarry, they are placed in a category distinct from that of the children of two brothers and two sisters, who are one another's brothers and sisters. In Thonga a boy calls his mother's brother's daughter 'mother', and she calls him 'son'. To be sure, the Baganda draw no distinction between the brother, the father's brother's, the father's sister's, the mother's brother's and the mother's sister's son. On the other hand, only the father's brother's daughter and the mother's sister's daughter are a man's sisters; his father's sister's and his mother's brother's daughter belong to the special category of *kizibwewe*, quite distinct from that of the sister, *mwanyina*.

To cut a long story short, all the evidence is opposed to Morgan's assumption that the Bantu systems are patterned on the Hawaiian principle of grading relatives by generations. There are merely occasional suggestions of that principle which will be discussed below as to their theoretical bearing.

So far as I know, there is only one region of the globe outside of Oceania and the possible Asiatic range defined above, where a definitely Hawaiian classification of relatives by generations has been reported, *viz.*, among the Yoruba of West Africa.[13] Unfortunately, no more recent check data for this section seem available. For another part of West Africa we have Mr. Northcote W. Thomas' tables,[14] which reveal a rather perplexing condition of affairs that seems to demand intensive reinvestigation together with linguistic analysis. The principle of bifurcation seems to hold sway only in a very limited measure.

Thus, the Vai do not distinguish the father's sister from the mother, though the mother's brother is designated by a distinct term from that for father and father's brother. Further, the term for child is extended also to brother's child by both sexes contrary to customary 'forked' usage. But this cannot be interpreted as symptomatic of the Hawaiian principle since the sister's child is designated by a special word, which, moreover, differs for men and women speaking. The Vai nomenclature is interesting in showing once more that a given 'system' is a complex growth that cannot be adequately defined as a whole by some such catchword as 'classificatory', 'Hawaiian', or what not. Not only do we find Hawaiian and Dakota elements in the same system, but even purely descriptive combinations of primary terms. Thus, the designation of the sister's daughter's husband is manifestly composed of the stems for sister's child and husband, and a corresponding juxtaposition of stems results in the term for mother's sister's husband.

A similar phenomenon is presented by the terminology of the Timne, another Sierra Leone people. A superficial glance at the list suggests the Hawaiian principle: father's brother and mother's brother are grouped together, and so are the children of the maternal and the paternal aunt. But closer consideration shows that while uncles are classed together they are sharply separated from the father, that while aunts form a single group of *ntene* the word for mother is *kara* or *ya*, that there is no connection between the words for *Geschwister* and cousins. In short, the Hawaiian generation principle does not apply.

What Mr. Thomas' schedules from eight tribes illustrate once more is the overwhelming importance of historical, geographical and linguistic considerations. A cursory examination of the lists shows that not only the mode of classifying kin but the words themselves are identical in a number of cases in two or more tribes. Thus, *mama* is grandmother in Karanko, Susu, Vai and Mendi. It is surely no accident that all of these belong to the same prefixless subdivision of the Sudanese languages: the similarity is due to historical relations. In some cases an identical word is shared by members of distinct subdivisions. Thus, the father's sister is called *ntene* not only in the non-prefixing Susu and Koranko speech, but also in the prefixing language of the Timne. A glimpse at Mr. Thomas' map shows, however, that the habitat of the Timne adjoins that of both of the other tribes; a kinship nomenclature is, in a measure, a function of geographical position.

The last-mentioned term is suggestive in another way. Restricted among the Koranko and Susu to the father's sister, it is applied by the Timne to the maternal aunt as well. Turning once more to the map, we discover that this latter mode of grouping, though not the same word phonetically, occurs among the Bulem, the immediate coastal neighbors of the Timne, who belong to the same linguistic subdivision, and also to the Mendi and Vai, to the east and southeast, who are members of the complementary subdivision. So far, this only indicates the spread of a terminological trait over a continuous area. But the data further suggest that the word *nlene* may have been borrowed by the Timne rather than in the reverse direction, and that, as Mr. Thomas himself remarks, the Timne secondarily extended the term to include a maternal as well as a paternal aunt. This possibility is theoretically significant, first, because it indicates that Hawaiian analogies may develop independently of any such generation principle as dominates the Oceanian system; secondly, because it suggests that such simplicity of nomenclature, instead of being primitive as Morgan supposed, may represent a later development. To this point we shall have to revert later.

The Dakota Principle. Let us now turn to that principle which first aroused Morgan's interest and which since his time has occupied perhaps more attention than any other, the classificatory principle *par excellence* in Dr. Rivers' opinion, which finds expression among such tribes as the Iroquois and Dakota. Like the Hawaiian principle, the Dakota alignment groups together, regardless of proximity of relationship, members of the same generation, but differs because in the speaker's generation, the first ascending and the first descending generations, it separates the paternal and the maternal line. Another way of expressing the facts is to say that collateral and lineal kin are merged irrespective of nearness of relationship but with strict bifurcation of the parental lines. Thus, in Dakota[15] the father, father's brother, father's father's brother's son, father's father's father's brother's son's son are all addressed *até;* the mother, mother's sister, mother's mother's sister's daughter are all called *iná*. So far we have a classing together of kin who in English are distinguished from one another. But there is separation of kin whom we class together, inasmuch as the mother's brother is designated by a term distinct from that for father's brother, *viz.*, by *dēkcí*, and the father's sister by a term differentiating her from the mother's sister, *viz.*, by *t 'uwí*. Now, relationship is a reciprocal phenomenon, and accordingly we may expect that all those whom I class together under the term *até* or *iná* will address me by a correlative term. Actually, we find that the Dakota have a single word, *mi tcíñkci*, for son, brother's son (man speaking), father's brother's son's son (man speaking), etc., and for sister's son (woman speaking), mother's sister's daughter's son (woman speaking). To put the matter into our own speech, for the sake of simplification, those whom I call father and mother call me son. If logic shall prevail, the data hitherto cited involve the condition that the mother's brother must not call his sister's son 'son', but shall designate him by some distinct appellation correlative only with the term *dēkcí;* and this holds for the Dakota system where a man (not a woman) calls the sister's son *mit 'úncka.* Further this term is also used by a woman addressing her brother's son, a point to which I shall have to return presently.

There are other logical implications in the features already mentioned. If the term for father embraces a number of other collateral relatives, we must expect a corresponding fusion of kin in the speaker's generation. This is exactly what happens. Like many other primitive systems, that of the Dakota classifies brothers and sisters according to relative seniority and the speaker's sex, but the same terms are applied to the other individuals who jointly designate the same members of the next higher generation as their fathers and mothers. In other words, a considerable number of cousins, irrespective of their varying degree, are classed with the brothers and sisters. But certain other cousins are *not* so classed: they are the offspring of the father's sister and the mother's brother. Corresponding exactly to the fact that sister's son (man speaking) and brother's son (woman speaking) are denoted by a single word, we have the correlative phenomenon that the children of the paternal aunt and the maternal uncle are relatives of a special order, the boys calling one another *t 'ahá ci* and the girls *hà kắ cí*, the girls calling one another *tcē̈ pqci* and the boys *citcé ci*.

In short, so far as the three middle generations are concerned, there is at least an approach to a real system—a unified logical scheme by which blood relatives are classified. If I am called father by a group of people, they are my sons or daughters; if I am their uncle, they are my nephews or nieces. In the former case, my sons and daughters are their brothers and sisters; in the latter my offspring are their cousins, with various refinements of nomenclature that are immaterial from a broader point of view.

The system is not perfect, because of the terminology applied to the offspring of cousins. As might be expected, a man regards the children of those cousins whom he classes with his brothers as brother's sons, *i.e.*, from the foregoing scheme, with his own sons. But contrary to what might be expected, he puts into the same category the sons of those male cousins designated by a distinctive term where we should expect a distinct correlative designation. Even Herr Cunow, who lays stress on the rational character of primitive relationship systems, is obliged to admit that there is inconsistency here.[16]

It cannot be too strongly urged that a given nomenclature is molded by disparate principles. It is, therefore, worth while to point out that the principle by which brothers and sisters are distinguished by seniority and the principle by which *Geschwister* of the same sex use different designations from those of opposite sex have no functional relation whatsoever with the principle by which collateral and lineal kin are merged. Another trait of the Dakota system which is similarly independent of what I call the Dakota principle is the differentiation in stem for vocative and non-vocative usage or with the first, second and third person. Thus, the mother is addressed as *iná*, but 'his mother' is *hų́ ku*, from an entirely different root. Passing to the second ascending generation, we find a Hawaiian feature inasmuch as the principle of bifurcation no longer holds, grandfathers of both sides being designated by a common term. The Dakota case once more shows that, as Professor Kroeber long ago pointed out,[17] every system is in reality a congeries of systems or categories which must be analytically separated unless complete confusion is to result. There is no Hawaiian *system*, no Dakota *system*. But we can legitimately speak of the principle of generations and the bifurcation principle of merging collateral and lineal kin; and we can speak, by conventional definition of the geographical terms employed, of Hawaiian and Dakota features to express these and only these elements of the Hawaiian and Dakota nomenclatures.

To revert to the Dakota principle, as Morgan points out,[18] the same principle has in part molded the Iroquois system, and when we find that in addition to the logically related elements the apparently irrational classification of cousins' offspring is likewise common to the two terminologies, the case for historical connection becomes very strong. This becomes a certainty when we find that in its essentials the principle finds expression in the system of the intermediate Ojibwa, while among other Algonkian tribes and among Siouan tribes other than the Dakota a marked variant from the Dakota type makes its appearance. In short, we have the Dakota principle spread over a continuous region, which is sharply separated from adjoining regions. It has, then, developed in a single center in this part of North America and has thence spread by borrowing.

If we ignore the mode of designating 'cross-cousins', *i.e.*, cousins who are children of a brother and a sister, and disregard certain other deviations constituting sub-types, we get a very much wider range of distribution for the Dakota principle in North America. The neglect of degree of kinship and the clear separation of the maternal and paternal line in the middle generations are features characteristic, probably, of the entire region east of the Mississippi and occur also in the Mackenzie River district, among the Tlingit and Haida of the Northwest Coast and most of the Plains tribes, in a part of the Pueblo territory (notably among the Hopi), and among the Miwok and adjacent populations in California. Since we are not by any means familiar with the kinship systems of the entire continent, it is necessary to supplement this statement with another indicating the regions where the Dakota principle is actually known to be lacking. The Dakota features are not found among the Eskimo, Nootka, Quileute, Chinook, various Salish tribes, the Kootenai, the Plateau Shoshoneans, nor in a large section of California to the north and east of the Miwok, and they are also absent from various Southwestern terminologies. The glib assumption of many writers that all of North America is characterized by a 'classificatory system' on the Dakota plan, is demonstrably false. The only reason for this belief is the historical accident that Morgan was conversant with the systems east of the Rocky Mountains and practically altogether ignorant of those of the Far West, and that since his time no one has systematically presented the data for what to him was a *terra incognita.*

Let us extend our search for evidences of the Dakota principle to other regions.

For Mexico, the data are not very satisfactory since we are obliged to rely on old Spanish sources and cannot be sure that our authorities were on the alert for differences from the familiar

European nomenclature or always correctly represented what they did find. Thus, Dr. Paul Radin, who has kindly compiled for me a Tarascan list from Gilberti's *Diccionario de la Lengua Tarasca* (1559), finds the children of the father's brother and of the mother's brother classed with the son and daughter (contrary to the generation principle), but distinguished from the children of the father's and mother's sister. This would indicate a departure from both the Hawaiian and the Dakota scheme. A bare suggestion of the latter is found in a common term for father and paternal uncle. The Nahuatl data supplied by Molina in his *Vocabulario de la Lengua Mexicana* (1571) show no difference between the paternal and maternal aunts and uncles. This does not apply to the Maya system reported by Beltran in his *Arte del Idioma Maya* (1742), but here the maternal and paternal uncle and aunt are not only distinguished from each other, but also from the father and mother, so that there is no merging of collateral and lineal lines in this generation. Accordingly, it is somewhat surprising to find that the children of a brother are classed with one's own children (male speaking?) and that a woman applies the same term to her sister's children, in accordance with Dakota usage. A very interesting feature of the Maya nomenclature is that differences in generation are conspicuously ignored in several instances. The paternal grandfather is classed with the elder brother, a single reciprocal term is used for daughter's son and mother's father, one word denotes the son's son and the younger brother.

For Central and South America the data, from a cursory inspection, seem somewhat more adequate, though we must eagerly await a more thorough-going survey of this region than can at present be offered. The Miskito of Nicaragua call the mother's sister *yaptislip*, which is merely a modification of *yapti*, mother, but while the father's brother, *urappia*, is classed with the step-father, he is distinguished from the father, *aisa*. At all events, there is a distinctive term for maternal uncle, *tarti*, and correlatively a special designation, *tubani*, for the sister's son (man speaking). For the father's sister our authority gives only a descriptive term: *saura* may be the correlative term, but it is simply translated 'brother's child'. Of the four terms for cousin, one is descriptive (child of brother or sister), two coincide with the regular words for *Geschwister*, the fourth is unfortunately not clearly defined so that its application to the cross-cousin, which would conform to Dakota usage, remains problematical. The terms of affinity are interesting inasmuch as the principle of reciprocity appears here. Thus, *dapna* means both father-in-law and son-in-law, and the same descriptive expression, oddly enough, is applied to the mother-in-law and daughter-in-law in female speech.[19] The former instance of reciprocity recurs among the Chibcha of Colombia and we may thus have here another case of the geographical localization of kinship features. The Chibcha list supplied by one of Morgan's informants,[20] imperfect though it is, records some suggestive facts. The term for father's brother seems only a variant of the word for father, and is clearly distinct from that for maternal uncle. The designations for both kinds of aunt are doubtful. In the speaker's generation 'parallel' male cousins, *i.e.*, the sons of two brothers and of two sisters, are grouped with brothers and distinguished from cross-cousins, as they are in the Dakota system. That a woman calls her father's sister's son by the same term as her husband is a fact of some theoretical importance since it suggests the possible occurrence of cross-cousin marriages.

From Martius' rather confusing Carib list we may reasonably infer that the paternal uncle was classed with the father in male speech and distinguished from the mother's brother. One of three terms used by a man in designating his son coincides with that applied to a brother's son, but differs from the word applied to the sister's son. These are Dakota features; and the peculiar statement that children of sisters were allowed to marry while those of brothers were not, coupled with the remark that *Geschwisterkinder* call one another brothers makes us suspect that we have here merely an abortive attempt to describe the difference between parallel and cross-cousins recognized on the Dakota principle. The Tupi terminology furnished by the same writer does not suggest the bifurcate feature. Though a single word denotes the father, his brother and other paternal kinsmen, it seems to extend likewise to the corresponding relatives on the mother's side. In the second ascending generation the grandfather's brothers and male cousins are classed with the grandfather—a Hawaiian trait if both sides of the family are meant to be included, but one common to most systems on the Dakota plan for the middle generations.[21] From the third great South American family I can get no satisfactory evidence of bifurcation on the Dakota plan. According to an accessible glossary of various Arawak tongues, the Siusi is the only language that discriminates between the paternal and maternal uncle, and even here the former is also distinguished from the father, so that there is no merging of collateral and lineal kin. Similarly, the word for aunt is different from that for mother; and here the principle of bifurcation is completely discarded, since a single word denotes father's and mother's sister.[22]

Bifurcation may be a dominant feature of systems which nevertheless differ markedly from the Dakota nomenclature because of their demarcation of collateral and lineal kin. Thus, the Araucanians of Chile call the father *chao*, the father's brother *malle*, the mother's brother *huecu;* the mother is *ñuque*, her sister *ñuquentu*, the father's sister *palu*.[23] Here the designation of the maternal aunt is clearly derived from that of the mother but we cannot tell whether this merging is an ancient feature which appears in other parts of the system or a recent development. We learn from another source that the brother's sons are differentiated from the sister's,[24] but unfortunately there is no statement as to whether the former in male speech and the latter in female speech are classed with one's own sons.

Bifurcation without reduction of the collateral lines is characteristic of the system of the Sipibo, who inhabit the country about the Ucayali River. Here the father is *papa;* the father's brother *eppa*, the maternal uncle *cuca;* the mother *tita*, her sister *huasta*, the paternal aunt *yaya*, and of the three words for brother's son (*pia*, *nusa*, *picha*) none even remotely resembles that for son, *baque.*[25]

To sum up the facts hitherto cited. If the doctrine of the unity of the American race depended on the uniformity of kinship terminologies in the New World, it would have to be mercilessly abandoned. Meager as are our data for the area south of the United States, we can find positive indications of nomenclatures with Dakota features only among the Caribs and the Chibcha, with occasional suggestions elsewhere. The Tupi and Arawak systems are markedly unforked; the Araucanian and Sipibo terminologies are forked but non-merging. Taking into account the large section of North America already defined as lacking bifurcation with merging, we thus have an immense territory in America in which the Dakota principle does not occur.

But, as the African facts cited above show, the Dakota principle is not confined to a portion of the Western Hemisphere. It is impossible completely to define its distribution in various parts of the globe, but the main regions must be indicated. As Morgan pointed out on the basis of Rev. Fison's information,[26] the principle occurs in the nomenclature of the Coastal Fijians, and corroborative evidence has recently been furnished.[27] Rivers has shown that the typical Dakota principle appears in other parts of Melanesia, often with a very interesting additional feature in the designation of cross-cousins, who are not only rigidly distinguished from the parallel cousins but classed simultaneously as brothers-in-law and sisters-in-law, *e. g.*, in Guadalcanar.[28] Bifurcation with merging of collateral and lineal relatives also characterizes at least some of the terminologies of New Guinea.[29] The same certainly holds for a large portion of Australia, though almost everywhere certain local refinements are apparent. Thus, the Urabunna apply one term to the father and the father's brothers, as might be expected. But instead of merely separating the mother's sisters from those of the father by grouping them with the mother, there is an additional dichotomy into the mother's elder sisters, *luka*, who are classed with the mother, and the mother's younger sisters who are differentiated as *nam-uma*. Corresponding differentiation occurs in the speaker's generation, where the father's elder sister's daughters are distinguished not only from parallel cousins but from the father's younger sister's daughters. Nevertheless, the essentials of the Dakota principle are manifest.[30]

Here it is worth while to point out again how misleading it is to treat accidentally associated features of a given system as functionally correlated. The Urabunna system, like that of other tribes, is not an organically unified whole. Thus, over and above the usual trait of bifurcate merging, we find the feature that a grandparent and grandchild use a common term in addressing each other. This reciprocity is often referred to as characteristic of 'classificatory systems'. It is nothing of the kind. In North America it occurs precisely in systems lacking the classificatory principle altogether. Apart from this, there is no manifest connection between the principles of grouping together relatives of alternate generations and the principle of classing under one head relatives of the same generation and side of the family. The mere fact that kinsfolk are united whom we happen to separate in nomenclature is a purely negative and insufficient reason for postulating an essential relationship between two modes of classification.

Finally, there are a number of Asiatic tribes whose systems reveal the essentials of the Dakota principle. At least a close approximation occurs in the nomenclature of the Gilyak of the Amur River country, where, except for the grouping together of father's and mother's sister, the two parental lines are kept apart while on either side the customary merging takes place.[31] The system of the Tamil, as Morgan emphatically pointed out, is almost identical with that of the Seneca Iroquois.[32] The essential resemblance to this type of the Toda,[33] Singhalese and Vedda[34] terminologies has since been established.

We are here again confronted by a problem in distribution that does not differ in principle from ethnological problems relating to other phases of culture. A sharply individualized feature is found not like the Hawaiian principle practically within the limits of a single continuous area but in several diverse and remote regions of the globe. It is impossible to hold with Morgan that the similarity found is an index of racial affinity unless we are willing to assume that the Indians of the eastern United States are not related at all to those west of the Rocky Mountains. The principle of diffusion obviously accounts for much. No one would hesitate to assume that the Singhalese and Vedda systems are connected and we should willingly regard both as historically related to the nomenclature of southern India. We might even be willing to grant that the Melanesian and Australian variants of the Dakota principle had the same source of origin. But how can we explain the predominance of the identical principle precisely in the eastern regions of North America and its absence in a great part of the Far West? And how can we account for the African approximations to the same pattern? We seem to have an independent evolution of the same highly characteristic trait in at least three distinct areas. Must we content ourselves with simply accepting the data as irreducible ethnological phenomena or can we carry our analysis a step further?

That the inclusiveness of terms which strikes us in the systems sharing the Dakota principle is somehow connected with the social divisions of the tribes concerned has been repeatedly noted. Even in his earlier, purely descriptive work Morgan remarked that among the Iroquois clan members were brothers and sisters as if children of the same mother.[35] Similarly among the Tlingit we are told that a single word is applied to the mother's sister and all other women of the same moiety and generation.[36] The Yakut apply one term to any woman older than the speaker and belonging to the same gens.[37] Such instances might easily be multiplied. It is therefore rather natural to look to a clan or gentile system for the explanation of the 'classificatory feature', *i. e.*, of bifurcate merging.

This hypothesis, which has recently been discussed by Swanton,[38] was already advanced only to be proved inadequate by Morgan himself. Taking the Seneca for illustration, where descent is in the maternal line, Morgan shows that the children of two sisters would indeed be members of the same clan and hence clan brothers and sisters but that this explanation no longer holds for the children of two brothers. By the law of exogamy these would be required to marry into another clan and there is no reason why their wives should belong to the same clan. Hence the brothers' children will not be clan brothers and sisters, yet, according to Seneca terminology, the offspring of brothers no less than of sisters are classed with own brothers and sisters. Accordingly, the clan system—though it has a definite place in Morgan's scheme of evolution—is not regarded by him as the determining factor of the Seneca-Dakota principle.[39]

But the objection vanishes if we accept the theory that the Dakota principle arose as a reflection not of a multiple clan system but of an organization with exogamous moieties. This theory, which to my knowledge was first developed by Tylor[40] and has since been advocated by

Rivers,[41] has obvious advantages. Even on the simple clan hypothesis it is clear why the father's brothers should be classed with the father and separated from the maternal uncles, since the latter by exogamy must belong to a different clan. The term which we translate 'father' would really be seen to mean 'male member of the father's clan and generation'. With the moiety theory the same facts are explained, but also in addition the designations for other relatives. To take again the Seneca instance, the sons of two brothers *must* be members of the same social division because with a dual organization the brothers are restricted to the same division in the choice of a mate; hence it is quite natural that the sons of brothers should call one another brothers. Again, the difference between parallel cousins and cross-cousins is perfectly intelligible. The mother's brother's and the father's sister's son can never be of my moiety; if descent is matrilineal they belong to my father's moiety, if patrilineal to my mother's. Hence it is natural that they should not be classed with my brothers who in either case are my moiety-mates. This hypothesis also explains features not yet referred to, but often found in conjunction with those grouped under the heading of the Dakota principle, *e. g.*, the frequent classification of the father's sister's husband with the maternal uncle. Given exogamous moieties, these relatives must belong to the same half of society, to my own moiety if descent is maternal, to my mother's if it is patrilineal. The Tylor-Rivers theory thus explains very satisfactorily the rather numerous features that jointly constitute what I have called the Dakota principle; we can at once see that here is not an arbitrary rule of classification but a definite rationale.

However, it is worth noting that while the moiety theory explains a number of traits better and more simply than the hypothesis of multiple clans or gentes of which it is a special form, the latter is not in so bad a plight as Morgan would have us believe. That I should call my father's brothers and male cousins of the paternal line 'father' and my mother's sisters and female cousins of the female line 'mother', follows from the general hypothesis of exogamy no less than from the moiety theory. The difficulty urged is the grouping together of brothers' sons who are not clansmen under a matrilineal organization with sisters' sons who are. But all terms of relationship are correlative: the concept of elder brother is meaningless without the correlated concept of younger brother; so the very fact that I address my father's brother as 'father' has as a necessary consequence that he should address me as 'son' regardless of whether his own son is in my clan. Similarly, the fact that my father's brother's son and I both address my own father as father makes us brothers irrespective of clan affiliation. Clan affiliation is still the primary determinant since it fixes the connotation of the word translated 'father', while the other usages mentioned are derivative applications. The objection that naturally obtrudes itself is why the term for father should be taken as the starting-point rather than that for son or brother. The answer lies in the fact that in a number of instances the term for father has an emphatically clan or gentile significance, being extended even to father's clansmen of the speaker's generation, as among the Crow and Arizona Tewa. Nevertheless, it cannot be denied that from the point of view of summarizing the data comprised under the caption of 'Dakota principle' or intimately linked with them the moiety theory is distinctly superior. Thus, the union of father's sister's husband and mother's brother under a single head does not follow from a multiple clan or gentile organization but is intelligible on the basis of a dual division.

The weakness of the moiety theory lies in another direction. In order that the dual organization may fashion kinship nomenclature, it must of course exist. Now it does occur in Australia and Melanesia, though not universally, and in part of North America, but it is lacking in many regions of this continent and, so far as I know, in Africa. If we derive the Dakota principle exclusively from the dual organization we are therefore obliged to assume either that this institution once had a far wider range of distribution or that the nomenclature it produced traveled independently of the moieties to a considerable number of other peoples. This is a difficulty that must be frankly recognized.

In this regard the exogamy hypothesis in the broader sense enjoys an obvious superiority. Exogamous kin groups occur both in southern Africa and in many sections of America from which exogamous moieties have never been reported. Doubtless here, too, we must reckon to a considerable extent with the effect of diffusion, which repeatedly carried the Dakota principle to non-exogamous tribes. Yet when we apply the method of variation to the best-studied regions of the globe, our confidence in the essential correctness of the exogamy hypothesis is considerably strengthened. In Oceania it is the non-exogamous Polynesians who fail to distinguish the maternal and paternal sides, while the generally exogamous Melanesians recognize the principle of bifurcation. In North America, the non-exogamous tribes are either bifurcating but fail to merge the collateral and lineal lines or neither bifurcate nor merge.[42]

Certain instances are especially illuminating because they permit a refinement of the method of variation by the practical or total elimination of other factors to account for the phenomena. Thus on the northwest coast of America we find certain tribes like the Kwakiutl and Nootka who are not organized in strictly exogamous groups, and here neither merging nor bifurcation occurs. "The terms for 'uncle' and 'aunt' refer equally to the father's and mother's fraternity;" and specific terms distinguish father and mother from more remote kindred. When we compare such systems with those of the more northern and exogamous tribes, *viz.*, the Tsimshian, Haida and Tlingit, we discover at once a striking difference. In all these terminologies men of the father's are distinguished from those of the mother's moiety or clan; and the collateral lines are wholly, or almost entirely, merged in the lineal lines.[43] Here we are not dealing simply with a contact phenomenon, for no good reason can be given why the Tlingit system should not have extended southward or the Kwakiutl system to the north. Nor are we simply confronted by a difference of tribal affiliation: while the Kwakiutl and Nootka belong to the same stock, and affinity has recently been claimed for the Tlingit and Haida languages, the Tsimshian stand apart. It is the difference in social organization that runs parallel with the difference in nomenclature.

A similar case is afforded by the Shoshonean stock. Within this family specific terms for father and mother as opposed to uncles and aunts are the rule and cross-cousins are generally not distinguished from parallel cousins and brothers. There is thus a combination of extreme Hawaiian inclusiveness in the speaker's generation with the tendency to non-classificatory nomenclature in the first ascending generation. But among the Hopi, the only member of the group organized into exogamous clans, the Dakota principle holds sway. Since no Southwestern system is known that so clearly reveals the forked and merging principle, the possibility of borrowing seems barred and we have proof of the independent evolution of this feature in correlation with a clan system.

So far, then, as the distribution of the Dakota principle over discontinuous regions of the globe is concerned, the hypothesis of exogamy gives a reasonably satisfactory explanation of the facts, while within each continuous area we shall assume a greater or lesser degree of dissemination. Applying this, *e. g.*, to the Northwestern Indians as a whole, we shall indeed regard the evolution of Dakota features as a response to the exogamous organization, but when we turn to the three exogamous tribes individually, we shall face the problem whether the terminology did not spread from one tribe to its two neighbors. It is quite true that theoretically there is the possibility that the *clan* system, not the terminology, was the diffused feature and that the organization in each case independently produced an appropriate nomenclature. However, we have undoubted instances in which features of nomenclature were not associated with any social institution, indeed, where the very words have been borrowed. Further the development of an appropriate terminology is not an absolutely automatic process, as is shown by the failure of some tribes with exogamy to develop one. Hence it seems probable that within a limited continuous area the Dakota principle developed only once and then spread to neighboring tribes.

That the existence of an exogamous organization among the borrowers would be a favorable condition for the adoption of the nomenclature is obvious, also that the organization and the terminology may be borrowed jointly.

In order to strengthen the case for the exogamous theory it is necessary to show that the same results could not be accomplished, or not so well, by other conditions of equally wide distribution. As a matter of fact, an alternative interpretation has recently been advanced.[44] In the case of the non-exogamous Californian Yahi Dr. Sapir connects the merging of lineal and collateral lines with the marriage regulations obtaining there and suggests that these rules "may no doubt not infrequently be examined as an equally or more plausible determining influence". The practices referred to comprise the levirate, *i. e.*, a man's marriage with his brother's widow, and marriage with the deceased wife's sister. (Why, *deceased?* we may well ask Dr. Sapir, since a man's preëmptive right to his wife's younger sisters is a widespread custom in North America.)

I do not doubt for a moment that the customs in question have affected kinship nomenclature, but I seriously question whether they constitute an adequate substitute for exogamy as an interpretation of the empirical distribution of the Dakota principle. The levirate, it is true, is an exceedingly widespread institution: Tylor found it among one hundred and twenty out of some three hundred peoples.[45] But the levirate alone will not do since it only explains the extension of the father term to the father's brother and the correlative extension of the term 'son' to the brother's son (man speaking). It remains to be seen, therefore, to what extent the levirate is united in different regions of the globe with the usage of marrying two or more sisters, which would further explain the classification of mother's sister with mother and of the sister's children with the children (woman speaking). So far as I know, the range of the two usages jointly has not been ascertained; pending its determination, the distribution of the Dakota principle is not accounted for, as it approximately is by exogamy.

There are certain other objections to the levirate hypothesis. One of them was already urged by Morgan, who examined it under the heading of polygamy and polyandry, which together might obviously lead to the same results as the Yahi usages.[46] These customs do not necessarily take in the entire population. A man may not have a brother to inherit his widow, nor have all women sisters to join or follow them in wedlock. On the other hand, clan or gentile affiliation is an automatic affair not touched by such contingencies.

Further, we may ask, what is really explained by the Yahi rules? The relationships of paternal uncle and maternal aunt and their discrimination from the mother's brother and father's sister are certainly accounted for; and correlatively, the distinction between the offspring of such relatives. But though discussion has hitherto for simplicity's sake been mainly restricted to these nearer kindred, the Dakota principle involves far more remote relatives. It is not only the father's brother but the father's father's brother's son and the greatgrandfather's brother's son's son that are classed with the father; not only the mother's sister but the mother's mother's sister's daughter and mother's mother's mother's sister's daughter's daughter that are classed with the mother. No doubt an explanation can be patched together on the levirate-polygyny hypothesis. Since my father is brother to my father's father's brother's son, the latter is my potential father under the levirate rule, and so forth. But even with the multiple clan or gentile hypothesis, the facts are more directly explained. From this point of view the relative in question is simply a father's clansman with paternal descent, while with matrilineal descent the designations for the mother's mother's sister's daughter *et al.* are at once clear. The moiety theory, of course, accounts for all the relevant data in the simplest manner.

It is, indeed, manifest that the levirate-polygyny rule stands to the exogamous principle somewhat in the relation of a part to the whole or of a special instance to a broader principle. Assume exogamous divisions, and my wife becomes *ipso facto* my brother's potential wife while my wife's sisters are my and my brothers' potential wives even though marriage be never actually consummated except monogamously. Incidentally, it is by no means certain that in reported cases the levirate is limited to the real brother or the multiple sister marriages to own sisters; indeed, in some cases the reverse is stated, cousins or members of the same clan or gens being expressly included. With the dual organization the case is especially clear. The kinship terms then appear simply as status names. I am brother to those who are potential husbands of the same group of women and since all of us males occupy this common status there is correlatively a single term by which all of us are called by our children. The status assumption is supported by such facts as the Gilyak rule by which men of a gens must take wives from a particular gens and where the gentes as units are regarded as standing to each other in the relationship of father-in-law and son-in-law.[47]

In short, where the levirate-polygyny usages coexist with exogamy, it would be rash to derive a merging and bifurcate nomenclature from the former rather than from the latter.

Still another objection is implied in Dr. Sapir's own statement of the case. It is not necessary for the natives to look at the levirate from the point of view hitherto assumed. Instead of defining the paternal uncle in terms of his potential fatherhood, they may have a word distinct from that for father to designate the stepfather and the paternal uncle. Dr. Sapir cites the Upper Chinook by way of illustration. In other words, the action of the levirate is equivocal. It may affect nomenclature so as to produce the semblance of the Dakota principle, but it may also produce quite different results. It may also fail to affect terminology at all, as apparently is the case in Semitic languages with their descriptive nomenclature.

In this connection a qualification must be made that applies equally to the exogamy hypothesis.

Though the ultimate cause of a terminological feature be the levirate, the immediate cause in a given instance may well be an historico-geographical one. If the Chinook nomenclature is differently affected by the levirate from that of the Yahi, the proximate reason may be simply the fact that the Chinook did not come into contact with the same peoples as the Yahi and thus had no chance to borrow their nomenclature. In other words, admitting an influence of the levirate, it is not necessary to assume that it has repeatedly produced the same terminological effects independently.

I know of at least one instance in which the hypothesis advanced by Dr. Sapir seems definitely excluded, leaving exogamy in the field as the efficient cause. The Hopi system conforms to the essentials of the Dakota type, but neither the levirate nor the marriage with two sisters is in vogue. It cannot be argued that the Dakota features were borrowed from some other Southwestern tribe possessing these usages, first, because the Dakota features are far more highly developed among the Hopi than among other Pueblo Indians; secondly, because it is very doubtful whether the practices in question occur among other Pueblo tribes.[48]

In justice to Dr. Sapir it must be pointed out that he does not advance his hypothesis as a general interpretation of the phenomena. As he suggests, it is most serviceable where the exogamous factor does not occur, or, as I should add, where diffusion of features from a system affected by exogamy seems improbable. I have examined his hypothesis as if it were designed to account for all the relevant phenomena simply in order to bring out clearly its inferiority from this point of view to the theory of exogamy.

There are two series of cases which strongly corroborate the theory of the effect of the exogamous organization on the kinship nomenclature. They constitute a distinct variant of the Dakota principle, the deviation being in the designation of cross-cousins. While these are still differentiated from parallel cousins, they are not placed together in a single category but are classed, one group of cousins with the first ascending and the complementary group with the first descending generation. In short, the generation factor which is fundamental in the Hawaiian scheme and only modified by dichotomy in the usual type of bifurcate merging schemes is here overridden by some other factor. Now what is the nature of this new determinant? Let us look at the facts.

The Hidatsa class the father's sister's son with the father and the father's sister's daughter and all her female descendants through females to infinity with the father's sister; correlatively, the mother's brother's son, in the absence of special words for nephew or niece, is classed with the son, even by women. That the Crow scheme is almost identical, is readily intelligible from the historical relations of the two tribes, who speak very similar languages of the Siouan stock. But the essentials of the classification reappear among the geographically, linguistically, and culturally remote Hopi, with suggestions of similar features among the Tlingit and even in Melanesia. We are again confronted with a puzzling problem of distribution.

An analysis of the Hidatsa data clarifies the situation. According to the statements of the natives themselves, the term 'father' is applied to any father's clansman irrespective of age and would accordingly include the father's sister's son. This suggests that the clue to the entire situation may lie in the clan feature. As a matter of fact, we find the daughter of the father's sister's *son* is not classed with the daughter of the father's sister's *daughter*. The only difference that can be connected with this distinction is that in clan membership: the former relative, owing to the exogamous clan system, can never, and the latter relative always must, belong to the father's sister's clan. Hence the former, being a father's sister's son's, *i.e.*, a 'father's', daughter, becomes in Hidatsa speech a sister, while the latter is designated by a word translated 'paternal aunt' but really embracing likewise all the lower generations of females in the paternal clan. That we are dealing with the clan factor, is corroborated by the fact that in Hidatsa terminology the mother's brother, instead of being designated by a specific word, is classed with the elder brother, a term also applied to the mother's mother's brother. The last-mentioned kinsman may be similarly addressed in Hopi.

Powerful corroborative evidence is supplied by a second series of facts. Among the Omaha, where descent is reckoned in the paternal line, the father's sister's daughter is no longer classed with the father's sister but with the sister's daughter. These, it may be noted incidentally, would belong to the same division if the moieties of the Omaha were at one time exogamous, for which there is some evidence. But the essential point is that here the mother's brother's son and all his male descendants through males are indiscriminately classed with the maternal uncle. It is clear that they are all members of the same gens, and corresponding to our Hidatsa experiment we find that as soon as we pass outside the gens the terminology changes: my mother's brother's *daughter's* son is not my maternal uncle but my brother since his mother, the uncle's daughter, is called 'mother', belonging as she must to my mother's gens.[49]

The Omaha phenomena are absolutely paralleled not only among other Southern Siouans but also among a number of Algonquians, *viz.*, the Miami, Sauk and Fox, Kickapoo, Menomini and Shawnee. The area covered is an absolutely continuous one, and it is impossible not to explain such a distribution by diffusion. This conclusion is accentuated by the fact that the Ojibwa, though an Algonquian people with a gentile system, do not share the Omaha variant of the Dakota scheme but conform to the more usual type found among their neighbors, the Dakota. The mere presence of a gentile organization, though doubtless a favorable basis for the development or adoption of the Omaha scheme, is not the only determining condition; the presence of terminological features in a particular tribe is also a function of its geographical position or historical connections. This does not interfere with the ultimate interpretation of such features but it shows the necessity of taking into account the geographico-historical situation. At present I cannot suggest what may have been the differential condition that produced the Hidatsa variant among some tribes with a clan system but not among the Iroquois; or the Omaha variant among certain Algonquian tribes but not the Ojibwa.

The exogamy hypothesis, with special reference, to the phenomena just mentioned, has recently been discussed by Professor Kroeber.[50] He accepts the empirical correlation between exogamy and the merging of lineal and collateral kin with bifurcation of the parental lines, but interprets it as due rather to the differentiation of male and female lines of descent than to exogamy itself, which latter he regards as 'perhaps a common but not necessary development, and an overlying development of the former'. "The basic condition," argues Dr. Kroeber, "would be that in which a woman would be felt to be a very different thing from a man in relationship—less perhaps as an existing individual than as a factor in the relations of other people. Once this point of view prevailed, cross-cousins would necessarily be felt to be something very different from parallel cousins, and cross-uncles and aunts from parallel ones;

and the distinction would find expression in nomenclature." Accentuation of the male and female lines of descent with greater weighting of the one would possibly lead to clan groups.

As a theory of the origin of exogamous groups I have no particular objection to offer to the foregoing. For reasons to be stated below (p. 163) I heartily concur in the assumption that the family, in America at all events, preceded the clan or gens. If I understand him correctly, Dr. Kroeber's remarks merely paraphrase the fact of this sequence. But I do not see that acceptance of his view on this point involves a rejection of the influence of the clan when that has once developed. Of course it is not directly exogamy that is expressed but the alignment in groups which exogamy brings about. On Dr. Kroeber's assumption it is unintelligible why father's sister's son and mother's brother's son should so frequently be classed together since the one is clearly related through the father, the other through the mother. We can hardly credit the native mind with a tendency to algebraic equalization of a plus and minus quantity by which the product of a male and a female relationship shall be standardized by a common designation. Generally speaking, Dr. Kroeber's factors explain only bifurcation but not merging.

The fact that even remote father's cousins are grouped with the father is what the clan or gentile hypothesis explains over and above the dichotomy of relatives. That such merging occurs among tribes with definite exogamous groups, and generally not in loosely organized ones, can hardly be an accident. Dr. Kroeber's case is, however, weakest as regards the Hidatsa and Omaha variants of the Dakota scheme. If 'unilaterality of descent' rather than clan or gentile affiliation is the determinant here, then why is the Hidatsa variant uniformly found among matrilineal tribes and the Omaha variant uniformly with a gentile system? In other words, why does not the Omaha call his father's sister's son 'father' and his father's sister's daughter 'aunt'? The cross-cousins in question are as clearly related to me through the father among the Omaha as among the Hidatsa, but in the former case they are not, and in the latter they necessarily are, my father's clansfolk. Similarly, the mother's brother's son and his male offspring are as emphatically related to me through my mother among the Hidatsa as anywhere, but they are not aligned in the same social group with one another and they are not classed together in terminology. For the sake of clearness I will, at the risk of repetition, formulate what I consider the probable course of events. Among certain loosely organized tribes the bifurcation of immediate kin evolved, as we find it among a number of our Far Western tribes. This tendency was amplified and became superseded by a definite clan or gentile scheme. As this scheme developed, possibly as a part of its growth, kinship terminology became not only forked but more inclusive as well. Finally, the fully established organization was able, in certain instances to exert the extreme retro-active influence on nomenclature revealed in the Hidatsa and Omaha variants.

In his extremely valuable paper on Miwok organization[51] Mr. Gifford also suggests a rival explanation in place of exogamy. The Miwok of California are organized in approximately exogamous moieties, and their nomenclature bears some resemblance to that of the Omaha. More particularly is the mother's brother's son (and his male descendants through males?) classed with the mother's brother. According to Mr. Gifford, this is due to the custom of a man marrying, either polygamously or after his wife's decease, the daughter of his wife's brother. This form of marriage is actually practised among the Miwok in addition to the more generally diffused marriage with the mother's brother's daughter. Obviously, the facts of terminology are consistent both with this usage and with the moiety principle. Mr. Gifford objects that among the Miwok "there are no clan or moiety brothers and sisters, all relationship being based on blood and marriage ties." This, however, is not the essential point. It does not matter whether the unrelated members are *called* brother or sister provided they are aligned together in the same social group; the very existence of such social groups implies a differential attitude towards fellow-members as compared with the rest of the tribe. That mere affiliation along moiety lines does not solve all the mysteries of Miwok terminology, is quite true since a sharp distinction is drawn between the mother's brother's daughter and the father's sister's daughter. Since both these relatives are eligible mates from the point of view of exogamy while as a matter of fact marriage with the paternal aunt's daughter is prohibited, Mr. Gifford's objection seems to be sustained. That is to say, here the social organization explains the classing together of certain relatives but not the exclusion of certain other relatives, while the specific marriage regulations of the tribe do account for this phenomenon. But on the other hand, the marriage rules fail where the moiety hypothesis succeeds. Why are the mother's younger sister, who cannot be married, and the father's brother's wife classed with the marriageable cross-cousin and the wife's brother's daughter unless it is because they are all members of the same moiety?

So far as the merging of a maternal uncle's male descendants through males with the uncle himself is concerned, I do not see how any marriage rule would directly explain the extension of the term *ad infinitum* while moiety alignment at once renders it intelligible. An advantage which the exogamous principle enjoys over every special marriage rule is the universality of its sway over the population. An individual's wife may not have a brother and her brother may not have a daughter for the husband to marry, but where exogamous groups exist every tribesman is by birth a member of a particular group.

To the subject of specific marriage rules I shall have to revert below. My position as to the Miwok nomenclature is that special regulations undoubtedly account for some of its features while the dual organization successfully explains others and more particularly the Omaha variant of the Dakota principle.

We may sum up our discussion of the Dakota principle with the statement that its distribution, coupled as it is with exogamous groups, supports the theory of an organic connection between the two phenomena. On the question which I have hitherto shelved, *viz.*, whether it is exogamy in any form or more particularly the dual organization that gave rise to the features under discussion, I am at present unable to reach a definite decision. Though the distribution of the moiety is far more restricted than that of exogamous groups generally, there is no doubt that not a few elements of the Dakota principle are most readily derived from a dual organization. It remains for the future to determine what is the relative part taken by the multiple kin group and the moiety organization in fashioning kinship nomenclature.

Before leaving the Dakota principle, it seems desirable to allude to two important theoretical problems with which it seems connected—its relations to the Hawaiian principle and its bearing on the antiquity of the clan organization. The Dakota scheme in its more usual form may be logically regarded as merely a complication of the simpler Hawaiian one. As Morgan pointed out, the two coincide in practically half of all the relationships. Inspired no doubt by the general trend of evolutionary thought in his day, Morgan converted the logical connection into an historical sequence and assumed the priority of the simpler system. He indicated how, if grafted on the Hawaiian scheme, the clan or gentile organization would transform it into the Dakota type. It does not seem to have occurred to him that the evolution might have taken place in the reverse direction. Development, as shown precisely by linguistic phenomena, such as the history of the English language —and kinship terms, no matter what else they may be, are elements of human speech— is not always from the simple to the complex. Morgan's belief was influenced by the view that humanity started their social existence at an extremely low level, for which opinion he found support in the social conditions he inferred from the Hawaiian schedules. These, he argued, suggest brother-sister marriage since such marriages would explain the use of the same term for mother's brother and father. Such unions certainly *would* produce the observed terminology but Morgan failed to consider that an alternative explanation was at hand. His fundamental error lay in attaching to the primary kinship terms of the Hawaiians and other peoples the notion of actual cohabitation. From this starting-point he consistently argued that all men addressed as father had actual access to the speaker's mother. As Cunow has well shown,[52] there is not a tittle of evidence that this represents the native point of view, from which the term 'father' merely indicates tribal status with reference to the speaker. When we have once recognized this fact, there is nothing so intrinsically primitive in the Hawaiian scheme of ranging kin as to demonstrate hoary antiquity.

All empirical considerations, indeed, point in the opposite direction. For one thing, all the peoples whose systems are characterized by the Hawaiian feature rank relatively high in the scale of civilization. No one would dream of placing the Maori culture below that of, say, the Fijians. Secondly, we have the most powerful circumstantial evidence from distinct quarters of the globe to prove that Hawaiian features develop secondarily within the Dakota scheme. Thus, among some Iroquois tribes, the tendency has developed to call the father's as well as the mother's sister 'mother'. The Crow differ from all other Siouan tribes, even from their closest relatives, the Hidatsa, in similarly extending the word for mother in direct address. Among the Torres Straits Islanders a corresponding change of usage was recorded by Dr. Rivers,[53] and similar developments seem to have occurred among the Gilyak.[64] Relevant data from West Africa have already been cited in another connection.

All this does not prove that as a general proposition Morgan's sequence must simply be inverted. For this there is no evidence in North America, where complete Hawaiian schemes, or even approximations thereto, are lacking. But the data at our disposal do indicate that in so far as a tendency toward Hawaiian elements appears it is often due to secondary development.

To turn next to the problem of the exogamous kin group. Some theoretical writers have assumed the priority of the clan or gens to the 'loose', *i. e.*, clanless or non-gentile, organization in which the family and local group usually form the only important social units. To support such a view appeals have sometimes been made to kinship nomenclatures. So far as North America is concerned, this argument is certainly without foundation. It was Dr. Swanton, I think, who first showed that in North America the exogamous system is found precisely among the more highly cultured tribes while generally speaking it is lacking among the more primitive peoples. Now as I have shown above, exogamy in North America largely goes hand in hand with the Dakota principle. It is therefore rather remarkable that the more primitive clanless North American tribes of the Plateau and neighboring regions also lack the Dakota principle. The suggestion sometimes offered that a clan or gentile system has once existed and simply eluded the field worker's scrutiny on account of the degeneration of aboriginal life under modern conditions thus breaks down. We cannot argue positively that where the Dakota principle reigns exogamy must necessarily have occurred, because the correlation, while high, is not perfect and because the principle may have been borrowed without the social organization. But an exogamous organization is so frequently associated with the Dakota principle and there is so little reason for a change of kinship terminology provided the native language is preserved that the total lack of Dakota features over a wide area may be regarded as exceedingly strong evidence against the former or at least ancient existence of exogamous groups.

Supposed Features of 'Classificatory' Systems. Under the misnomer 'classificatory systems' some writers have included consideration of the principle of differentiating elder and younger brothers and sisters. The distribution of this distinction is simply staggering when one attempts to trace it more or less systematically. Of North American systems, I can offhand recall only two, the Pawnee and Kiowa, in which it does not appear. We find it in association with the Hungarian and Chukchee terminologies, both of which lack the Dakota principle, and it occurs with the Hawaiian no less than the vast majority of bifurcate systems. So far as I know, the only one who has offered any explanation of the phenomenon is Dr. Rivers, who once connected it with a difference in the time of tribal initiation.[55] But since there are many peoples, *e. g.*, in North America, who do not practise any form of tribal initiation, the hypothesis hardly seems tenable and we must rest content to accept the facts of distribution.

Another feature that is often erroneously treated in association with the Dakota principle is that of reciprocity, which has already been referred to as the usage of designating a pair of relatives, more particularly two belonging to different generations, by a single term. Thus, the Shoshone call the mother's father and the daughter's son (man speaking) by one term. Such usage would be manifestly opposed to the Hawaiian principle with which it does not seem to be associated. It is found in connection with the Dakota scheme in Melanesia and particularly in Australia, but is markedly absent from the merging systems of North America. Since here it is highly developed where the Dakota principle does *not* occur, it cannot be regarded as an essential element of 'classificatory systems'. The question remains how we are to account for the facts of distribution. Australian data forcibly suggest that, there at least, the reciprocal feature is a reflection of social organization. Grandparents and grandchildren, by the curious rule of descent that regulates affiliation with the matrimonial classes of the area, are necessarily in the same class, *i. e.*, a father's father and a son's son or a mother's father and a daughter's son (man speaking) are fellow-members of a class. The fit seems too close to admit of an accidental association. But when we turn to the North American region of reciprocal features the interpretation no longer holds since no vestige is found there of any institution that might align the relatives under discussion in a common group. The inference is that there has been convergent development, and perhaps the most plausible explanation of the North American terms is that they are designations not so much of the relatives as of the relationship itself.[56]

If we cannot give more than this general interpretation of the reciprocal feature as found in North America, we can on the other hand show quite definitely that its occurrence is a function of geographical position there. The practical absence of this trait in the immense region particularly dealt with by Morgan is as remarkable as its spread over a practically continuous region in the Far West, among the Lillooet, Spokane, Kootenai, Nez Percé, Wishram, Takelma, and various Californian and Shoshonean Plateau populations, as well as in a considerable number of Southwestern tribes. The Pacific, Plateau and Southwestern regions obviously define the distribution of reciprocity in North America, which thus becomes intelligible only through diffusion.

Various Features. The principles of kinship nomenclature that have been treated hitherto are far from exhausting the variety found in a survey of the world. A very odd mode of addressing relatives after presentation of a gift has been mentioned for the Masai (p. 104), and there is little doubt that more extensive knowledge will reveal equally quaint notions elsewhere. Here I merely wish to enumerate a few examples from the particular point of view assumed in this chapter.

It is a remarkable fact that while in Australia the principle of bifurcation is consistently carried to the grandparental stratum of society in conjunction with the reciprocal feature, the North American region in which the Dakota principle is especially prominent lacks the distinction between mother's and father's parents, so that Morgan does not even dedicate special columns to these relationships in his elaborate schedules and notes the discrimination with some surprise for the Spokane.[57] This feature is nevertheless widely spread in the Far West, coinciding to some extent with that of reciprocity. We find it among Salish and Shoshonean tribes, in California, among the Takelma and Wishram, and to some extent in the Southwest. Both the positive and the negative facts of distribution indicate the occurrence of diffusion.

The change of terms after the death of a connecting or other relative is another feature of considerable interest. Thus, the Kawaiisu of California address the father as *muwuni*, but by the quite distinct term *kuguni* after the loss of a child.[58] Again, the Kootenai have one word for the father-in-law before and another after the wife's or husband's death. This peculiarity appears also among Californian tribes, the Chinook, Quileute, and several Salish tribes.

This distribution again demonstrates diffusion from a common center. On the other hand, the probably even higher development of *post-mortem* nomenclature among the Timucua of Florida[59] cannot be ascribed, in the present state of our knowledge, to anything but independent origin, though we are not in a position to state what common cause, lacking in the intervening area, produced the common effect in the southeastern United States and in the remote regions of the Far West.

I will only call attention to one other kinship usage of more general interest, that embraced in the term 'teknonymy', the custom of denoting an individual in terms of his relationship to a child, *viz.*, 'father of Mary', 'grandmother of John'. This practice exists in South Africa and India,[60] in Melanesia,[61] and in the Pueblo area and on the Northwest coast of North America.[62] Tylor connected it with the custom of the husband's residence with his wife's kin, of the father's assertion of his paternity and his ultimate recognition as more than a stranger by the wife's family with whom a condition of ceremonial avoidance obtains. However, it should be noted that among the Zuñi and the Hopi, though the husband lives with his wife's people, there is no parent-in-law taboo, and the wife is as often referred to teknonymously as the husband. Thus, my Hopi interpreter always spoke to me of his wife as 'Herman's mother'. Tylor's explanation is accordingly inadequate and would seem to require at least amplification. But whatever result a systematic survey of the subject may lead to, it is certain that the effect of diffusion will have to be taken into account. It is inconceivable, *e. g.*, that the practice originated independently among tribes so geographically situated and so intimately related in culture as the Zuñi and Hopi.

Special Forms of Marriage and Social Customs. There can be little doubt that a well-established marriage rule often finds expression in nomenclature. Even the exogamous principle can be brought under this head since it expresses the potential matrimonial status of members of the community. In a dual organization my 'father' is one who potentially, if not actually, is a mate of women of my mother's group, while a 'mother's brother' is one who can under no condition occupy that status.

Of the specific forms of marriage the levirate has already been considered and the cross-cousin marriage briefly mentioned. Dr. Rivers has demonstrated the close dependence of nomenclature on the latter practice in Melanesia. Here the custom itself is found in full swing, and it would be unreasonable to deny that the terminology had its origin in this usage even in parts of Melanesia where it cannot be observed. This does not mean that cross-cousin marriage necessarily obtained throughout the range of distribution of the corresponding terminology but that the terminology spread from a center where it reflected the social institution. Thus, in Guadalcanar the cross-cousin marriage still persists and we find cross-cousins, brothers-in-law and sisters-in-law comprised under a single appellation. In Anaiteum, cross-cousins of opposite sex address one another by the terms used for husband and wife.[63] It seems to me methodologically quite justifiable to interpret similar features in neighboring islands as having their ultimate origin in cross-cousin marriage. But the argument fails where similar connotations of terms occur without evidence of the marriage rule unless it can be demonstrated that no other cause could have produced the result. Thus, I must consider unsuccessful Dr. Rivers' attempt to deduce, though with qualifications, the former existence of the institution in question from the system of the Dakota Indians.[64] The classification of brothers-in-law with cross-cousins might be simply a reflection of the dual organization, by which these relatives would fall within the same group; or, to put it differently, if the term cross-cousin is given the wide significance with which we are familiar in primitive systems, so as to include members of the opposite moiety and one's own generation, a man's brothers-in-law are necessarily members of the cross-cousin class. The superiority of the moiety hypothesis in this instance lies in the fact that the dual organization occurs among several contiguous and related tribes while the cross-cousin marriage is extremely rare in North America and its highest development occurs among remote peoples of the Pacific region. Regarding special forms of marriage, it is rather important to ascertain whether the terms used by our authorities are to be interpreted in our own or in the more inclusive primitive sense. For example, Tylor reduced the institution of cross-cousin marriage to the principle of exogamous moieties by assuming the wider significance.[65] As Dr. Rivers points out,[66] the two rules are not identical if marriage is prescribed with the own daughter of the own mother's brother. In that case, the moiety rule is only a larger framework with which the specific institution is not incompatible but which does not determine cross-cousin marriage. Looking at the matter chronologically, I can even conceive the development of larger social groups from such specific marriage regulations. If in the absence of an own cross-cousin, a more remote cousin comes to be regularly substituted, we should have a whole class of possible mates, of whom the nearest cross-cousin would be only *primus inter pares.*

It must be understood that while special marriage regulations, like exogamy, tend to be mirrored in nomenclature, there is no absolute necessity for this occurrence. As the New Mexican Tewa have exogamous groups without the Dakota principle, so the Miwok of California have the cross-cousin marriage with little or no indication of it in terminology.[67] One factor that must always be considered in this connection is the time element. A recently acquired custom may not yet have developed an appropriate nomenclature, while, as Morgan supposed, the nomenclature may survive after the custom has become obsolete. That the frequency of marriage according to a certain rule, and the coexistence of other rules, possibly antagonistic in their effects, must have an influence, is obvious. As regards the latter point, Mr. Gifford shows that while marriage with the cross-cousin is not suggested in Miwok nomenclature, marriage with the wife's brother's daughter is reflected by twelve terms.

Among the Thonga of South Africa several interesting forms of preferential matrimonial union occur. As among the Miwok, marriage with the wife's, younger sisters and wife's brother's daughter is considered peculiarly appropriate, and these affinities are subsumed under a common caption. Levirate extends only to the elder brother's, not to the younger brother's, wife, and quite consistently these affinities are distinguished by distinct words. A man may inherit his maternal uncle's wife and therefore classes her with the wife. On the other hand, logic does not hold sway undisputedly. A man calls cross-cousins by the same term as parallel cousins and brothers, yet it is possible for a man to inherit his parallel cousin's, but not his cross-cousin's (father's sister's son's), wife. The explanation given by Junod seems quite satisfactory from a comparative point of view. My cross-cousin cannot belong to my gens, my parallel cousin must belong to it.[68] Since the Thonga usually distinguish marriage potentialities with considerable nicety, we may reasonably infer that the present terminology for cousins is a recent innovation, which conclusion once more indicates the relatively late development of Hawaiian features.

A systematic comparison of the effect of definite forms of marriage on nomenclature, in different parts of the world is highly desirable. When we shall have examined how such an institution as the inheritance of a maternal uncle's wife affects the systems of the Tlingit of northwestern America, of the Banks Islands in Melanesia, and the Thonga of South Africa, and know the action of whatever coexisting institutions may occur, we shall have gained considerably more insight into a very suggestive problem. It is fairly clear that a form of marriage does not determine nomenclature univocally, as the facts relating to the levirate indicate. To ascertain in how far parallelism actually occurs, is a matter of great moment.

Conclusion. The question with which this chapter opens has now received an answer. Terms of relationship form a proper topic of investigation for the ethnologist, first because they are often directly correlated with cultural phenomena, such as social usages regulating marriage; secondly, because the features of kinship nomenclature are an index of tribal relationship. Any particular system is not a unified logical whole but a complex product of internal development and foreign connections. Accordingly, its features cannot be understood by themselves any more than other cultural phenomena, but only in association with concomitant traits of the native culture and in the light of a comparative survey of like features among neighboring tribes and ultimately throughout the world. By utilizing our ethnographical knowledge in applying the method of variation it is possible to ascertain, at least to a considerable extent, the causes, whether primary or secondary, that have shaped a given system.

When, for example, we endeavor to explain the system of the Hopi, we can start with the fact that their speech constitutes them a member of the Shoshonean family, *i. e.*, we can begin by comparing Hopi nomenclature with that of the Paiute, Paviotso, Ute and Shoshone. One fact that strikes us here is the great difference in the actual vocables employed by the Hopi from those of their congeners, an observation which by no means extends to all of their language. Morgan held the view that kinship words were the most persistent elements of speech, but however this rule may work in other stocks, such as the Athabaskan, it certainly does not obtain among the Shoshoneans, nor, I may add, within the Siouan family, where even such closely related languages as Crow and Hidatsa reveal far greater differences in the lexicon of relationships than might be expected from other vocables. It is, however, in the classification of kin that the distinctiveness of the Hopi seems most remarkable. Their system is not characterized by the prominent features of the Plateau Shoshonean terminologies, such as reciprocity and the separation of paternal from maternal grandparents. On the other hand, they employ the Dakota principle with the Hidatsa variation, That variant occurs, so far as we now know. only among peoples historically quite unrelated to the Hopi so that neither genetic connection nor dissemination accounts for the similarity. On the other hand, all the tribes having this feature share exogamous groups with maternal descent. Such clans are characteristic of the Hopi also, but are lacking among the other Shoshoneans. We infer from this that the Hidatsa variant among the Hopi is functionally connected with their clan system. If the neighboring Zuñi do not share this characteristic, a possible explanation may be found in the relative weakness of the Zuñi clan concept, as recently expounded by Professor Kroeber, when contrasted with its dominance in the social life of the Hopi. In other features the intimate cultural contact between the Zuñi and Hopi is emphatically apparent. Probably for no other tribes is there evidence for such exaggerated reliance on teknonymy, while a certain looseness in the use of terms common to both seems to be a general Southwestern trait. The Hopi system thus reflects both the social fabric of the tribe and its historical relations,—the ancient ones reduced to a few lexical resemblances, while the more complex tribal organization and recent cultural affiliations with the Southwest, and particularly with the Zuñi, stand out in bold relief.

A strictly similar inquiry might be made into the system of the Crow. Here the almost complete coincidence of certain very unusual features with Hidatsa ones bears eloquent testimony to the exceptionally close genetic relationship of the two tribes. Thus, a wife who has been married before is distinguished by a specific word, and spouses generally refer to each other not by a specific term, which seems restricted to non-vocative usage, but by a demonstrative expression. Not only is there a confusion of generations according to the Hidatsa variant, but the mother's brother is classed with the elder brother and so is the mother's mother's brother. The last-mentioned features are partly found among the Mandan. All three tribes differ from the other Siouans, and indeed from all other Plains Indians in having matrilineal descent. Since this is likewise the rule among genetically unconnected peoples sharing the Hidatsa variant, we regard the latter as functionally connected with the clan organization. But there are other traits in which the terminology of the Crow differs from that of their nearest congeners, and here we must systematically consider the possible effect of all such peoples as the Oglala, or Blackfoot, with whom they have come into contact. Such divergence may be merely the effect of internal readjustment. Thus, the Crow classification of the father's sister's husband with the father admits of a plausible interpretation as the result of another peculiarity—the classing of the father's sister with the mother in direct address. Instead of having two deviations from the Hidatsa norm, we should thus have at bottom only one.

It is clear that a far more intensive investigation of kinship terminologies must take the place of what has hitherto been attempted. Precisely the so-called minor peculiarities of a system are important historically because they are the differential indications of cultural contact with definite tribes. The phonetic inadequacy of Morgan's schedules, which has been brought to light by Dr. Michelson and Mr.

Spier,[69] requires a reëxamination of the entire field covered. Still more important is the thorough-going determination of the innumerable systems, both in and outside of America, not touched upon by Morgan at all. Fortunately the work of Dr. Rivers, Mr. A. R. Brown and Mr. A. M. Hocart in England, of Dr. R. Thurnwald in Germany, of Dr. J. R. Swanton, Mr. Leslie Spier and Mr. E. W. Gifford in America bids fair to reduce our ignorance of the facts. With our lamentable absence of knowledge on some of the most essential points it would be rash indeed to claim for the present sketch a more than preliminary value. I am content with calling attention to the tremendous ethnological significance of kinship terminologies, with combating premature confidence in generalizations based on sheer ignorance, and above all with suggesting that the most rigorous logical formulation of problems is possible in this too long neglected domain of the science of culture.

REFERENCES

I

1. WISSLER, CLARK. Psychological and Historical Interpretation for Culture, *Science*, N. S. vol. 43, pp. 193–201, 1916. HOCART, A.M. Psychology and Sociology, *Folk-Lore*, 1915, pp. 115–137. KROEBER, A. L. Eighteen Professions, *American Anthropologist*, N. S. vol. 17, pp. 283–288, 1915. LOWIE, ROBERT H. Psychology and Sociology, *American Journal of Sociology*, 1915, pp. 217–229.
2. RADLOFF, WILHELM. Aus Sibirien. Lose Blätter aus meinem Tagebuche. 2 vols. Leipzig, 1893, vol. 2, p. 16 f.
3. JOCHELSON, WALDEMAR. The Yukaghir and Yukaghirized Tungus, *Memoirs, American Museum of Natural History*, vol. 13, part 1, Leiden and New York, 1910, pp. 30–38. CZAPLICKA, M. A. Aboriginal Siberia. A Study in Social Anthropology. Oxford, 1914, pp. 307–325.

II

1. THORNDIKE, EDWARD L. Mental Work and Fatigue and Individual Differences and their Causes. New York, 1914, pp. 206–224.
2. MAXIMILIAN, PRINCE OF WIED. Reise in das innere Nord-Amerika in den Jahren 1832 bis 1834. Coblenz, 1841, vol. 2, p. 134.
3. LAUFER, BERTHOLD. Some Fundamental Ideas of Chinese Culture, *Journal of Race Development*, vol. 5, 1914, pp. 160–174.

4. LAUFER, BERTHOLD. Zur Geschichte der Brille, *Mitteilungen zur Geschichte der Medizin und der Naturwissenschaften*, vol. 6, 1907, pp. 379–385.
5. THORNDIKE. *op. cit.*, p. 223.
6. LAUFER, BERTHOLD. Skizze der mongolischen Literatur, *Extrait de la Revue Orientale*, 1907, pp. 165–261, esp. p. 232 f.
7. LAUFER. *Ibid.*, pp. 183–187
8. LAUFER, BERTHOLD. Skizze der manjurischen Literatur, *Extrait de la Revue Orientale*, 1908, pp. 1–53, esp. pp. 12 f., 17 f. GILES, H. A. The Civilization of China, *Home University Library*, London, 1911, p. 209.
9. HELL, J. Die Kultur der Araber, Leipzig, 1909, pp. 68, 93, 97, 83 f., 89, 99, 100.
10. GILES. *Op. cit.*, p. 119.

III

1. WISSLER, CLARK. The Psychological Aspects of the Culture-Environment Relation, *American Anthropologist*, N. S., vol. 14, 1912, pp. 217–225. WISSLER, CLARK. The Relation of Culture to Environment from the Standpoint of Invention, *Popular Science Monthly*, 1913, pp. 164–168. BOAS, FRANZ. The Mind of Primitive Man. New York, 1911, pp. 160–164. GOLDENWEISER, A. A. Culture and Environment, *American Journal of Sociology*, 1916, pp. 628–633.
2. OBERMAIER, HUGO. Der Mensch der Vorzeit. Berlin, no date, p. 238 f.
3. BOGORAS, WALDEMAR. The Chukchee—Material Culture, *Memoirs, American Museum of Natural History*, vol. 11, part 1, Leiden and New York, 1904, p. 7, *et seq.*

4. RADLOFF, WILHELM. Aus Sibirien, vol. 1, p. 444 f.
5. LAUFER, BERTHOLD. *Journal of Race Development*, vol. 5, pp. 167-170.
6. MORICE, A. G. The Canadian Dénés, *Annual Archaeological Report*, 1905, *Appendix, Report, Minister of Education*, Toronto, 1906, pp. 187-219, 197 f.
7. BOAS, FRANZ. The Eskimo of Baffin Land and Hudson Bay, *Bulletin, American Museum of Natural History*, vol. 17, 1907, pp. 75, 357.
8. FORRER, ROBERT. Urgeschichte des Europäers von der Menschwerdung zum Anbruch der Geschichte, Stuttgart, 1908, p. 197.
9. BOAS, FRANZ. Mind of Primitive Man, p. 162. BOGORAS, The Chukchee, p. 177.
10. RIVERS, W. H. R. The Disappearance of Useful Arts, *Festskrift tillägnad Edvard Westermarck*, 1912, pp. 109-130.
11. NELSON, N. C. Chronology of the Tano Ruins, New Mexico, *American Anthropologist*, N. S., vol. 18, 1916, pp. 159-180.
12. JOCHELSON, WALDEMAR. Material Culture and Social Organization of the Koryak, *Memoirs, American Museum of Natural History*, vol. 10, part 2, 1908, p. 405.
13. WISSLER, CLARK. Aboriginal Maize Culture as a Typical Culture-Complex, *American Journal of Sociology*, 1916, pp. 656-661.

IV

1. RIVERS, W. H. R. Kinship and Social Organization, London, 1914, p. 92.
2. TYLOR, EDWARD B. Primitive Culture; Researches into the Development of Mythology, Philosophy,

Religion, Languages, Art and Custom. 2 vols., New York, 1889, vol. 1, p. 53.

3. HATT, GUDMUND. Moccasins and their Relation to Arctic Foot-Wear, *Memoirs, American Anthropological Association*, vol. 3, no. 3, 1916, p. 246.
4. WISSLER, CLARK. Aboriginal Maize Culture, etc., pp. 656–661.
5. BOAS, FRANZ. Mind of Primitive Man, p. 167.
6. MONTELIUS, O. Der Handel in der Vorzeit, *Praehistorische Zeitschrift*, II, 1910, pp. 249–291; *Id.*, A Guide to the National Historical Museum, Stockholm.
7. FORRER, ROBERT. Urgeschichte des Europäers, etc., p. 197.
8. LAUFER, BERTHOLD. Chinese Pottery of the Han Dynasty. Leiden, 1909, pp. 212–236.
9. OBERMAIER, HUGO. Der Mensch der Vorzeit, p. 337.
10. BOAS, FRANZ. Mind of Primitive Man, p. 182 *et seq.*
11. WISSLER, CLARK. Material Cultures of the North American Indians, *American Anthropologist*, N. S. vol. 16, 1914, pp. 447–505, pp. 487–489.
12. CZEKANOWSKI, JAN. Objektive Kriterien in der Ethnologie, *Korrespondenzblatt der Deutschen Gesellschaft für Anthropologie, Ethnologie und Urgeschichte*, 1911, XLII, pp. 71–75.
13. TYLOR, E. B. On a Method of Investigating the Development of Institutions; applied to Laws of Marriage and Descent, *Journal of the Anthropological Institute*, vol. 18, 1889, pp. 245–272, esp. p. 264.

V

1. MORGAN, LEWIS H. Systems of Consanguinity and Affinity, *Smithsonian Contributions to Knowledge*, vol. 17, Washington, 1871, pp. 463 *et seq.*, 508.

2. SKINNER, ALANSON. Social Life and Ceremonial Bundles of the Menomini Indians, *Anthropological Papers, American Museum of Natural History*, vol. 13, part 1, 1913, p. 40. MORGAN, LEWIS H. Systems (Winnebago and Dakota), p. 181.

3. MERKER, M. Die Masai, Ethnographische Monographie eines ostafrikanischen Semitenvolkes, Berlin, 1904, pp. 41–43.

4. ROSCOE, JOHN. The Baganda, an Account of their Native Customs and Beliefs, London, 1911, pp. 130–132.

5. RIVERS, W. H. R. Kin, Kinship, *Hastings' Encyclopædia of Religion and Ethics.*

6. MORGAN, LEWIS H. Systems, p. 12.

7. RIVERS, W. H. R. The History of Melanesian Society, 2 vols., Cambridge, 1914, vol. 1, p. 375 *et seq.*

8. MORGAN, LEWIS H. Systems, pp. 457–461. ERDLAND, P. A. Die Marshall-Insulaner; Leben und Sitte, Sinn und Religion eines Südsee-Volkes. Münster in W., 1914, p. 114 f.

9. RIVERS, W. H. R. Kin, Kinship.

10. MORGAN, LEWIS H. Systems, pp. 463–466.

11. ROSCOE, JOHN. The Baganda, pp. 126–132. SCHINZ. Deutsch-Südwest-Afrika, Oldenburg, 1891, pp. 175–178. JUNOD, HENRI A. The Life of a South African Tribe. Neuchâtel, 1912–1913, vol. 1, pp. 217–237.

12. JUNOD, HENRI A. *Op. cit.*, pp. 237 f, 253–257.

13. ELLIS, A. B. The Yoruba-speaking Peoples of the Slave Coast of West Africa. London, 1894, pp. 177–182.

14. THOMAS, NORTHCOTE W. Law and Custom of the Timne and other Tribes, Anthropological Report on

Sierra Leone, London, 1916, p. 103 *et. seq.*, and tables.

15. MORGAN, LEWIS H. Systems, p. 167 *et. seq.*, also author's notes.
16. CUNOW, H. Zur Urgeschichte der Ehe und Familie (*Ergänzungshefte zur Neuen Zeit*, Stuttgart, 1912), p. 65.
17. KROEBER, A. L. Classificatory Systems of Relationship, *Journal of the Royal Anthropological Institute of Great Britain and Ireland*, 1909, pp. 77–84.
18. MORGAN, LEWIS H. Systems, pp. 167–169, 205.
19. ZIOCK, H. Dictionary of the English and Miskito Language. Herrnhut, Saxony, 1894.
20. MORGAN, LEWIS H. Systems, p. 265.
21. MARTIUS, CARL FRIEDRICH PHIL. V. Beiträge zur Ethnographie und Sprachenkunde Amerikas, zumal Brasiliens. Leipzig, 1867, vol. 1, pp. 353–355.
22. KOCH-GRÜNBERG, THEODOR. Aruak-Sprachen Nordwestbrasiliens und der angrenzenden Gebiete, *Mitteilungen der Anthropologischen Gesellschaft in Wien*, XLI, 1911.
23. BÜRGER, OTTO. Acht Lehr- und Wanderjahre in Chile. Leipzig, 1909, p. 86.
24. MEDINA, JOSÉ TORIBIO. Los Aborijenes de Chile. Santiago, 1882, p. 280 f.
25. VON DEN STEINEN, KARL. Diccionario Sipibo. Berlin, 1904.
26. MORGAN, LEWIS H. Systems, pp. 570–572.
27. RIVERS, W. H. R. The History of Melanesian Society, vol. 1, pp. 266–271.
28. RIVERS, W. H. R. *Ibid.*, vol. 1, p. 244.
29. ZAHN in NEUHAUSS, R. Deutsch-Neu-Guinea. 3 vols., Berlin, 1911, vol. 3, p. 304 f.

30. SPENCER, BALDWIN, and GILLEN, F. J. The Native Tribes of Central Australia. London, 1899, p. 66.

31. CZAPLICKA, M. A. Aboriginal Siberia, p. 98 f. VON SCHRENCK, L. Reisen und Forschungen im Amur-Lande. St. Petersburg, 1891, vol. 3, p. 236.

32. MORGAN, LEWIS H. Systems. pp. 387, 508.

33. RIVERS, W. H. R. The Todas. London, 1906, pp. 483–494.

34. SELIGMANN, C. G. and B. Z. The Veddas. Cambridge, 1911, p. 64.

35. MORGAN, LEWIS H. League of the Ho-dé-no-sau-nee or Iroquois. New York, 1904, Book 1, Chap. 4.

36. SWANTON, JOHN R. Social Conditions, Beliefs, and Linguistic Relationships of the Tlingit Indians, *Twenty-sixth Annual Report, Bureau of American Ethnology*, Washington, 1908, p. 424.

37. CZAPLICKA, M. A. Aboriginal Siberia, p. 60.

38. SWANTON, JOHN R. Significance of the Terms for Brother and Sister among Primitive Peoples, *Journal of the Washington Academy of Sciences*, 1917, pp. 31–35.

39. MORGAN, LEWIS H. Systems, p. 476.

40. TYLOR, E. B. Journal of the Anthropological Institute, vol. 18, 1889, p. 262 f.

41. RIVERS, W. H. R. Kinship and Social Organization, p. 73.

42. LOWIE, ROBERT H. Exogamy and the Classificatory Systems of Relationship, *American Anthropologist*, N. S., vol. 17, 1915, pp. 223–239.

43. BOAS, FRANZ. Tsimshian Mythology, *Thirty-first Annual Report, Bureau of American Ethnology*, Washington, 1916, pp. 489–495.

44. SAPIR, EDWARD. Terms of Relationship and the Levirate, *American Anthropologist*, N. S., vol. 18, 1916, pp. 327–337.

45. TYLOR, E. B. Journal of the Anthropological Institute, vol. 18, 1889, p. 253.

46. MORGAN, LEWIS H. Systems, p. 478 f.

47. CZAPLICKA, M. A. Aboriginal Siberia, p. 99.

48. KROEBER, A. L. Zuñi Kin and Clan, *Anthropological Papers, American Museum of Natural History*, vol. 18, 1917, p. 90.

49. DORSEY, J. O. Omaha Sociology, *Third Annual Report, Bureau of American Ethnology*, Washington, 1884, p. 254. MORGAN, LEWIS H. *Systems*, p. 335 f.

50. KROEBER, A. L. Zuñi Kin and Clan, p. 86 f.

51. GIFFORD, E. W. Miwok Moieties, *University of California Publications in American Archæology and Ethnology*, vol. 12, no. 4, Berkeley, 1916, p. 187 f.

52. CUNOW, H. Die Verwandtschafts-Organisationen der Australneger, Stuttgart, 1894, p. 127 f.

53. RIVERS, W. H. R. Kinship, *Reports, Cambridge Anthropological Expedition to Torres Straits*, vol. 2, p. 98.

54. STERNBERG, LEO. The Turano-Ganowanian System and the Nations of Northeast Asia, *Proceedings, International Congress of Americanists*, 18th session, 1912, pp. 319–333.

55. RIVERS, W. H. R. On the Origin of the Classificatory System of Relationships, *Anthropological Essays presented to Edward Burnett Tylor*, pp. 309–323.

56. RIVERS, W. H. R. The History of Melanesian Society, vol. 1, p. 8 f.

57. MORGAN, LEWIS H. Systems, p. 247.

58. GIFFORD, E. W. Tübatülabal and Kawaiisu Kinship Terms, *University of California Publications in American Archæology and Ethnology*, vol. 12, no. 6, Berkeley, 1917, p. 229.

59. SWANTON, JOHN R. Terms of Relationship in Timucua, *Holmes Anniversary Volume*, Washington, 1916, pp. 451–463.

60. TYLOR, E. B. Journal of the Anthropological Institute, vol. 18, 1889, p. 248.

61. RIVERS, W. H. R. The History of Melanesian Society, vol. 2, p. 336.

62. KROEBER, A. L. Zuñi Kin and Clan, p. 72. LOWIE, ROBERT H. Field Notes. KRAUSE, A. Die Tlinkit Indianer, Ergebnisse einer Reise nach der Nordwestküste von Amerika und der Beringstrasse im Auftrage der Bremer Geographischen Gesellschaft, 1880–1881, Jena, 1885, p. 217.

63. RIVERS, W. H. R. The History of Melanesian Society, vol. 2, p. 27.

64. RIVERS, W. H. R. Kinship and Social Organization, pp. 49–52.

65. TYLOR, E. B. Journal of the Anthropological Institute, vol. 18, 1889, p. 264.

66. RIVERS, W. H. R. History of Melanesian Society, vol. 2, p. 122.

67. GIFFORD, E. W. Miwok Moieties, p. 190.

68. JUNOD, HENRI A. The Life of a South African Tribe, vol. 1, pp. 247–250.

69 MICHELSON, TRUMAN. Notes on the Piegan System of Consanguinity, *Holmes Anniversary Volume*, Washington, 1916, pp. 320–333. SPIER, LESLIE, Blackfoot Relationship Terms, *American Anthropologist*, N. S. vol. 17, 1915, pp. 603–607.